Revision Guide
to A2 Level
Economics

James Keefe and **Peter Cramp**

anforme

ISBN 978-1-905504-32-9
Anforme Ltd, Stocksfield Hall, Stocksfield, Northumberland NE43 7TN.
Typeset by George Wishart & Associates, Whitley Bay.
Printed by Potts, Cramlington.

Contents

The first pages you will come to offer advice on using this book. After this, you will find revision notes organised as shown below:

Unit 3:
(Micro)

AQA – Business Economics and the Distribution of Income
Edexcel – Business Economics and Economic Efficiency
OCR – Economics of Work & Leisure or Transport Economics*

Unit 4:
(Macro)

AQA – The National and International Economy
Edexcel – The Global Economy
OCR – The Global Economy

*This book includes the key concepts and theories that you will need for the OCR Unit 3 options, but you may wish to supplement your revision using other books set in the relevant contexts. For Work & Leisure, try Labour Markets (4th edition): The Economics of Work and Leisure by Peter Cramp (Anforme).

Using this book

This book provides revision notes for both your A2 Economics units. It assumes that you already understand the key concepts and theories from AS level. The Revision Guide to AS level Economics (Peter Cramp & James Keefe), is also available from Anforme.

For each unit, the relevant chapters follow a defined structure. It is important that you understand this structure.

Unit 3 – Structure	
Introductory concepts	Costs and revenues; efficiency and equity; profits and objectives of firm.
Markets generally work well	Price Mechanism: Competitive markets allocate resources efficiently through the forces of supply and demand, setting the relative prices of goods. Contestable markets may also function well.
Sometimes markets fail	Market failure occurs when markets fail to produce desirable outcomes, either because the allocation of resources is not efficient or because the outcome is unfair (there is a lack of equity).
This may justify government intervention	Governments may respond to market failure by intervening to improve the resource allocation or produce a more equitable outcome.
Government failure sometimes occurs	Government intervention is not always effective in achieving its aims. The costs of intervention may exceed the benefits, creating a loss of economic welfare. This is government failure.

The Unit 3 chapters essentially follow this structure. Each chapter has a bar at the top showing the above structure and highlighting where the particular chapter fits into this structure. For example, Chapter 4 is about Competitive Markets and helps to understand why markets generally work well and allocate resources efficiently. 'Markets generally work well' is therefore highlighted within the structure:

Chapter 4

Unit 3: Introductory concepts → **Markets generally work well** → Sometimes markets fail → This may justify government intervention → Government failure sometimes occurs

Competitive markets

If a particular chapter crosses over more than one bit of the structure, the relevant parts of the structure are all highlighted.

The notes for Unit 4 (macroeconomics) also follow a defined structure:

	Unit 4 – Structure
Measuring the macroeconomy	The main four macroeconomic objectives (strong and sustainable growth, low unemployment, low and stable inflation and a satisfactory current account of the balance of payments) and their measurement were covered at AS level. These A2 notes pay particular attention to measurement of living standards, economic development and sustainability.
How the macroeconomy works	The circular flow of income and aggregate supply/aggregate demand analysis were covered at AS level.
Macroeconomic performance	Understanding the demand and supply side factors that influence performance with regard to the four main economic objectives. The difference between factors that affect the short run performance of the economy and the fundamental supply side determinants of long run performance.
Macroeconomic policy tools	Fiscal and monetary policies as ways of influencing aggregate demand and stabilising the economy. Supply side policy as a tool to influence trend growth and long-term economic performance.
International economics	The economics of international trade, protectionism, exchange rates, globalisation, trading blocs, monetary union, economic development and sustainability.

The chapter headings also work in the same way for Unit 4 as they did in the first section of the book. For example, the chapter on Living Standards, Development and Sustainability is about 'Measuring the macroeconomy' so this is highlighted:

Chapter 16

Unit 4: **Measuring the macroeconomy** → How the macroeconomy works → Macroeconomic performance → Macroeconomic policy tools → International Economics

Living standards, development and sustainability

It may be helpful for you to have the specification (syllabus) for your exam board with you when you revise. We have tried to ensure that the relevant concepts and theories on your specification are included in the book. If you are following OCR's specification you might choose to supplement this book with notes applying the Unit 3 theory to the specific content of the option you are studying which will be either 'The Economics of Work and Leisure' or 'Transport Economics'.

Where it is useful to do so, we have included specific guidance at the start of a chapter about its relevance to a particular specification. So, for example, Chapters 13-15 are not needed for Edexcel's Unit 3 course. However, Edexcel students may still find these chapters interesting. You can never know too much Economics!

We wish you good luck with your revision programme and your exams.

James Keefe and **Peter Cramp**

Chapter

1

Unit 3: Introductory concepts → Markets generally work well → Sometimes markets fail → This may justify government intervention → Government failure sometimes occurs

Costs and Revenues

The activity of firms	Firms combine **factors of production** (land, labour, capital and enterprise) into **output** (goods and services). The production of output results in costs for the firm, but the sale of output generates revenue. Costs relate to the supply side of a market, while revenue relates to demand.
Costs of production	An economist measures the firm's production costs as the **opportunity cost** of the factors of production used (the revenue that the factor could have generated in its next best use).
Short run	This is the period of time in which at least one factor of production is **fixed** (usually capital). Labour is typically regarded as a **variable factor**.
	It is impossible to put an actual length of time on the short run. A market trader may be able to buy a new stall and hire a new pitch in a day; a firm producing nuclear power could take a decade to build a new power station.
Long run	This is the period of time in which all factors are variable in quantity and in which it is possible for the firm to move to a new scale of production.
Marginal product of labour	The marginal product of labour is the additional output produced by adding one extra worker (a variable factor) to a given stock of fixed factors. This is the only way in which output can be increased in the short run.
Gains from specialisation	As more labour is added to a stock of fixed factors, the marginal product of labour tends to rise at first, due to gains from specialisation (extra workers more fully utilise available capital and make the **division of labour** possible).
	More specifically, the gains from specialisation are:
	● Workers can be assigned to tasks to which they are well suited.
	● Workers 'learn by doing' and efficiency improves through experience.
	● Production line methods eliminate the need to change tools and this saves time.
	● Production line methods may make it cost effective to provide specialist capital equipment for workers.
Diminishing marginal returns	Eventually the gains from specialisation are exhausted and, at some point, the additional output from employing extra workers begins to diminish.
	The **law of diminishing returns** states: "As more workers are added to a given stock of fixed factors, first the marginal product of labour and then the average product will eventually decline".
Average product of labour	The average product of labour is simply the total output divided by the number of workers used.

The shape of the marginal and average product curves

In Figure 1.1, gains from specialisation shape the rising sections of the average and marginal product curves, before diminishing returns set in.

Figure 1.1: Average and marginal product curves

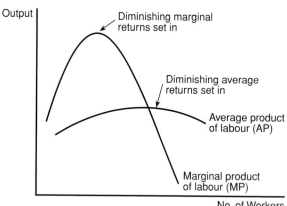

Fixed costs

These are costs that do not vary with output. They must be paid in the short run even if no output is produced. Examples include the rent on premises, which must be paid until the existing contract expires.

Variable costs

These are costs that vary in proportion to the output. Examples might include electricity and gas costs.

Total costs

The total cost of production (TC) consists of the total fixed costs (TFC) plus total variable costs (TVC): TC = TFC + TVC.

Average costs

Average fixed cost (AFC) is simply the total fixed cost (TFC) divided by quantity of output produced (Q): AFC = TFC/Q.

Average variable cost (AVC) is the total variable cost (TVC) divided by quantity: AVC = TVC/Q.

Average (total) cost (AC) is the total cost divided by the quantity produced: AC = TC/Q. Since TC consists of TFC and TVC, this is the same as AC = (TFC + TVC)/Q or AC = AFC + AVC.

Marginal cost

Marginal cost (MC) is the additional cost of making one extra unit of output.

The shape of short run cost curves

An extra unit of output can only be produced in the short run by adding more of a variable factor, typically labour. The marginal cost of producing an extra unit of output rises when the marginal product of labour falls: the marginal cost curve is the mirror image of the marginal product curve. Marginal cost reaches its bottom point as marginal product peaks.

Similarly, the average variable cost curve is the mirror image of the average product of labour.

This in turn means that short run cost curves are shaped by initial gains from specialisation as more labour is added to a given stock of fixed factors, and then by the onset of diminishing returns to labour.

Average fixed costs fall continuously as more output is added because a constant total fixed cost is spread over more units of output.

Average cost, like average variable cost, initially falls due to gains from specialisation but later rises under the influence of diminishing returns. However, it takes longer to rise than average variable cost. This is because AC = AFC + AVC and the continuously falling average fixed costs exert some downward pressure on AC even after diminishing returns set in.

Figure 1.2: Average and marginal cost curves

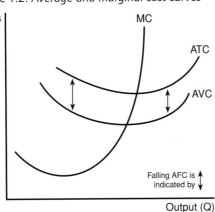

It is important to note in Figures 1.1 and 1.2 that the marginal curves go through the average curves at the highest or lowest points of the average curves. Mathematically, if the marginal is above the average, then the average must rise, but the average will fall if the marginal is below the average. Consider, for example, a cricketer's batting average. If a batman's average is 50 and he scores 60 in his next (marginal) innings his average will rise. If he scored only forty in his next (marginal) innings then his average would fall.

Long run production and returns to scale

In the long run, all factors of production are variable. When a firm increases output it can increase all the factors of production (land, labour and capital).

● **Increasing returns** to scale occur when the % change in output > % change in inputs.

● **Decreasing returns** to scale occur when the % change in output < % change in inputs.

● **Constant returns** to scale occur when the % change in output = % change in inputs.

Increasing returns to scale influence the long run average cost curve (see the next section) by creating economies of scale; decreasing returns to scale are associated with diseconomies of scale.

Long run average costs

In the long run, the scale of production can be increased, or reduced, as all factors are variable. This allows the firm to move on to new average cost curves. For each size of firm there is an equivalent short run average cost curve. As the firm expands its output it moves on to different short run average cost curves. In this example, it would move from AC1 to AC2 to AC3. If expanding the scale of output leads to a lower average cost for each level of output, then the firm is said to be experiencing economies of scale. This is illustrated in Figure 1.3.

Figure 1.3: Long run average costs

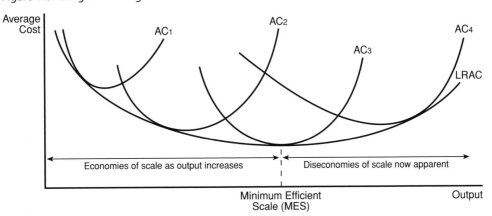

The points of tangency on the long run average cost (LRAC) curve do not occur at the minimum points of the SRAC curves except at the point where the **minimum efficient scale** (MES) is achieved. This is the minimum level of output required to exploit fully economies of scale.

Internal economies of scale	Internal economies of scale result from the growth of the firm itself and are usually categorised into technical economies, marketing economies, managerial economies, financial economies and risk-bearing economies.

Technical economies

These relate to the production and distribution process. Examples include:

● Larger firms can employ and combine specialist machinery that should reduce the average costs of production. For example, a large supermarket could install bar code technology which would reduce the average cost of recording and ordering stock. It would not, however, be economically viable for a small corner shop to buy this technology.

● Within larger firms there is also greater scope for the **specialisation of labour**, reducing AC. The production line in many car plants is a good example of this concept.

● The law of increased dimensions. Doubling the height and width of a tanker or building can lead to a more than proportionate increase in the cubic capacity. Examples of industries where this is important include: food retailing, hotels, motor manufacturing, oil & gas distribution, airlines, transportation, warehousing & storage.

Marketing economies

These relate to buying and selling. As a firm grows in size it can spread its advertising budget over a larger output but, most importantly, it can purchase its factor inputs in bulk at negotiated discounted prices. A large firm may have **monopsony (buying) power**. Supermarkets have used their power to drive down the cost paid to suppliers, e.g. British farmers.

Managerial economies

These arise as a result of the application of the **division of labour** to management. For example, larger supermarkets can afford to employ specialist buyers who can reduce buying costs. Better management and the use of specialist equipment, such as networked computers that improve communication, raise productivity and reduce average costs.

Financial economies

Larger firms normally have greater access to credit facilities, with favourable rates of borrowing in comparison to smaller firms.

Risk-bearing economies

As firms grow, they may be able to reduce costs by effectively self-insuring. For example, product diversification reduces the risk associated with the failure of any one product because the firm can be sustained by more successful lines of output.

External economies of scale

External economies of scale arise from the growth in the size of the industry as a whole. Firms within the industry will experience a fall in long run average costs, particularly if the firms are clustered in one geographical region. The firm's entire long run average cost curve shifts downwards as the industry grows. One example of an external economy of scale is when component suppliers for an industry start to set up in business. If these firms specialise in the production of supplies for the industry, they may be able to attain internal economies of scale which will **reduce the unit cost of components** for the industry. Component suppliers will certainly be able to produce parts at a cheaper cost than if individual firms tried to make them themselves.

Diseconomies of scale

Diseconomies of scale arise when the firm grows beyond the scale of production that minimises average cost. Examples include:

● **Control** – monitoring how productive each worker is in a modern corporation is both imperfect and costly.

● **Co-ordination** – it is difficult to co-ordinate complicated production processes and they may break down. Achieving efficient flows of information in large businesses is expensive.

● **Co-operation** – workers in large firms may feel a sense of alienation. If they do not consider themselves to be an integral part of the business their productivity may fall.

Revenue

Revenue is the income generated from the sale of a good or service. The revenue earned by a firm depends on the willingness of consumers to buy the product at any given price and therefore relates to demand.

Total Revenue

The total revenue earned from sales of a product can be measured by its price (P) multiplied by the quantity (Q) sold: TR = P x Q

This can be illustrated as the area under the demand curve, as shown in the first part of Figure 1.4.

Figure 1.4: Total revenue

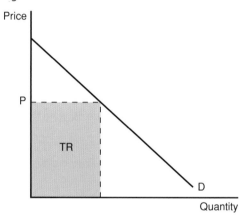 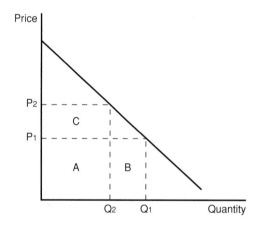

In the second part of Figure 1.4, we see how total revenue changes when prices increase from P1 to P2. At price P1, total revenue is Area A + Area B. When the price rises to P2, a contraction of demand means that Q2-Q1 units are no longer sold, resulting in a loss of revenue equal to Area B. However, the price rise increases the revenue gained on the Q2 units that are still sold by an amount equal to Area C.

Whether total revenue increases, decreases or stays the same following a price increase depends on **price elasticity of demand** (PED). If demand is elastic, a more than proportionate contraction in demand occurs which will more than cancel out the positive effects on total revenue of a price rise. Area B will be greater than Area C and total revenue will fall. If demand is inelastic, total revenue will rise. If demand has unitary elasticity, total revenue will be unchanged.

	PED > 1 (elastic)	PED < 1 (inelastic)	PED = 1 (unitary)
Price rise	TR falls	TR rises	TR constant
Price fall	TR rises	TR falls	TR constant

Marginal revenue

Marginal revenue (MR) is the addition to revenue from selling one extra unit of the good or service.

Average revenue

Average revenue (AR) is the total revenue divided by quantity sold: AR = TR/Q.

Since TR = P x Q, we can also state average revenue as AR = (P x Q)/Q, which reduces to AR = P. The average revenue from the sale of each unit of a product is simply the price for which that product sells. Because the demand curve tells us the price at which any given quantity can be sold, it also tells us the average revenue for that quantity and so the demand curve and the average revenue curve are one and the same thing.

Revenue curves

In Figure 1.5 the demand curve (AR curve) facing the firm is **perfectly elastic**. As the firm sells each additional unit at a constant price, AR must equal MR. The total revenue curve is a straight line because marginal revenue is both positive and constant. This situation applies to firms that are price takers, operating in highly competitive markets (see Chapter 4).

In Figure 1.6, the firm faces a downward sloping demand curve. This situation applies to a firm with some degree of monopoly (**price making**) power (see Chapter 5). To sell an extra unit of the good, the firm must reduce the price, including the units that it would have sold at the existing price. This means that marginal revenue from the sale of the extra unit is less than the price (which is equal to average revenue) for which it is sold. Thus the MR curve lies below the AR curve.

It can be mathematically proven that the MR curve is always twice as steep the AR curve. Total revenue is maximised when MR is zero and the elasticity of demand is equal to 1. This is the exact mid-point of a straight line demand curve extending from one axis to the other (mathematically, elasticity is infinity where the demand curve touches the vertical axis and zero where it cuts the horizontal axis). Up to point A, MR is positive so any increases in output result in a rise in total revenue. Beyond this point MR is negative and any rise in output causes a fall in total revenue.

Figure 1.5: Price takers

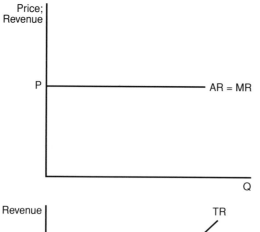

Figure 1.6: Price makers

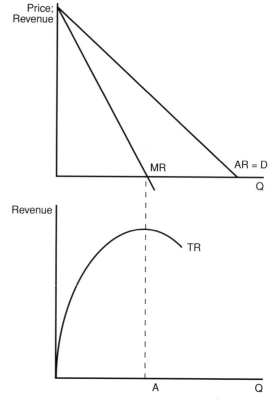

Chapter

2

Unit 3: **Introductory concepts** → Markets generally work well → Sometimes markets fail → This may justify government intervention → Government failure sometimes occurs

Efficiency and Equity

Economic efficiency

Economic efficiency concerns the relationship between the **inputs** to the production process (land, labour, capital and enterprise) and the **output** they produce.

This concept is at the heart of economics, which is about the basic problem of resources that are **scarce** in relation to infinite needs and wants. The central purpose of economic activity is the creation of utility (benefit) by the satisfaction of wants and needs. Society must make choices about how best to use its scarce resources. This implies a need to produce at the lowest possible cost and to allocate resources to the uses in which they produce most utility.

Efficiency is a concept that belongs to the field of positive economics (the economics of fact and testable hypotheses).

Technical efficiency

Technical efficiency involves producing a given quantity at the lowest possible average cost.

All points on the long run average cost curve (LRAC) are technically efficient. The LRAC represents a boundary between those output/cost combinations which are attainable and those which are not.

Figure 2.1: Long run average cost

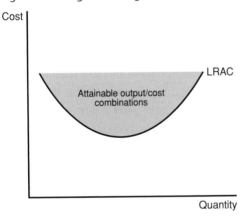

Technical inefficiency (x-inefficiency)

Technical inefficiency is more commonly known as **x-inefficiency**. It occurs when there is waste in the production process, so that the average cost for producing a given level of output is higher than it need be. All points above the LRAC exhibit x-inefficiency.

There are many reasons why x-inefficiency might occur. Possible explanations include:

● Weaknesses in the organisation of production and management.

● Lack of competition, allowing firms to survive without striving to reduce costs.

● A lack of a **profit motive**. It is often argued that state owned firms tend to be inefficient for this reason, while private firms have an incentive to bear down on costs.

● A **divorce of ownership and control** (see Chapter 3 for more detail). Unless the owners of a firm (typically the share holders) are able to hold the management of a firm effectively to account, the firm may fail to minimise costs. Managers may adopt **satisficing** behaviour and only work to reduce costs to the level necessary to produce enough profit to satisfy shareholders.

X-inefficiency is illustrated in Figure 2.2, where output Q is produced at average cost AC_A when it could be produced at a cost as low as AC_B.

Figure 2.2: X-inefficiency

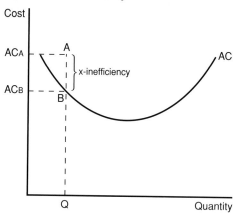

Productive efficiency

Productive efficiency entails producing goods and services at the lowest possible average cost for *any* level of output.

It is achieved when the average cost curve is at its bottom point and implies that all available internal economies of scale are being exploited.

Although the LRAC curve is traditionally drawn as u-shaped, so that there is only one level of output for which minimum average cost is achieved, there are other possible shapes for the curve. It is likely that many real world firms could achieve the lowest possible average cost at a range of different output levels before diseconomies of scale set in. This would imply a curve like the one on the right in Figure 2.3.

Minimum efficient scale

The minimum efficient scale (MES) of production is the smallest scale of production that allows the exploitation of all internal economies of scale and hence production at the lowest possible average cost. The MES varies from industry to industry. It may be quite small in service industries which have little capital equipment, such as cleaning firms. However, it is likely to be quite large in capital intensive sectors where there are many technical economies of scale available, such as car manufacturing.

Figure 2.3: Possible shapes for the long run average cost curve

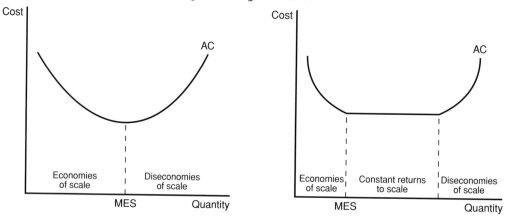

Allocative efficiency

Allocative efficiency is achieved when society derives the most possible utility from its scarce resources.

The concepts of **technical** and **productive efficiency** are *not* related to whether people gain utility from the goods and services produced. It would be possible to produce video recorders with no waste and at the lowest possible average cost, but this would be irrelevant if no consumers wanted video recorders. It would be more efficient to allocate those resources to making DVD or Blu-ray players if there is a greater demand for these products.

Allocative efficiency and the cost-benefit principle

The concept of allocative efficiency is best understood using the cost-benefit principle. It is worthwhile allocating resources to producing an extra unit of a good if the marginal benefit (utility) of doing so exceeds the marginal cost.

The price that a consumer is willing to pay for a good is a measure of the benefit or utility that they receive from it. In Figure 2.4, all consumers receive a **consumer surplus** (they would have been willing to pay more for the good than they actually pay), except the last (marginal) consumer who was willing to pay exactly price P. Thus the demand curve, by telling us the price associated with any given quantity, also tells us the marginal benefit (MB) derived by the last consumer.

The price that a firm is willing to supply a good for is an indication of the cost of producing it. In Figure 2.4, all units supplied except the last (marginal) unit carried a **producer surplus** (producers would have been willing to supply these units for less than the price they actually received). The last unit is supplied at exactly the price that producers needed to encourage them to supply it. Thus by showing us the price necessary to encourage any given level of supply, the supply curve also shows us the marginal cost (MC) of producing an extra unit.

Figure 2.4: Allocative efficiency

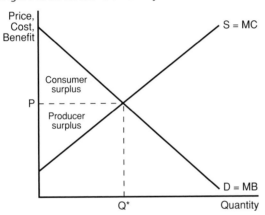

Applying the cost-benefit principle, we can see that all units produced up to Q* improved resource allocation because they carried a greater marginal benefit than cost. The opposite would be true of any units produced beyond Q*: they would create a net loss of welfare.

It is worth remembering the economist's definition of production costs here: the **opportunity cost** of all factors of production used is measured as the revenue that they would have generated in their next best use. When marginal benefit is greater than marginal cost this means that making a unit of the good in question is the most productive use (in terms of utility) for the resources required to make that extra unit.

At Q*, MB = MC. Since the demand curve tells us both the price and the marginal benefit associated with any given quantity, the condition for allocative efficiency can be restated as: **P = MC**.

Q* can also be referred to as **socially optimal**.

This analysis assumes that there are no positive or negative externalities associated with production and consumption. Properly speaking, the marginal benefit should perhaps be referred to as the marginal private benefit (MPB) and the marginal cost as the marginal private cost (MPC).

Allocative efficiency (social optimality) where there are externalities

The following two equations are vitally important:

Social benefit = Private benefit + external benefit

Social cost = Private cost + external cost

When there are no externalities associated with the good, social and private costs and benefits are one and the same thing. However, when there are externalities, the condition for allocative efficiency (social optimality) must be amended. **Externalities** are third party effects not accounted for in market prices.

Applying the cost-benefit principle when externalities are present results in the conclusion that allocative efficiency (social optimality) is achieved when: **MSB = MSC**.

Social optimality is achieved at Q* in Figure 2.5.

Figure 2.5:

Positive externalities   *Negative externalities*

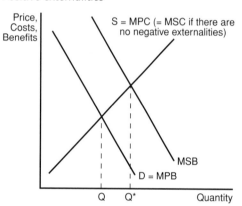
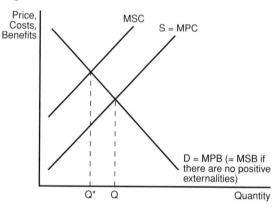

Static vs. dynamic efficiency

Allocative, technical and productive efficiency are **static** concepts, concerned with efficiency at a specific point in time. **Dynamic efficiency** is concerned with the future. It may be dynamically efficient to devote resources to research and development, because of the positive effects that they can have on future standards of living.

Equity

Equity can be understood to mean fairness. In contrast to efficiency, it is a concept that belongs to normative economics (it involves value judgements or opinions). Market performance is typically evaluated both from a **positive** perspective of efficiency and a **normative** perspective of equity.

Horizontal and vertical equity

Horizontal equity is concerned with the fair treatment of people whose circumstances are the same (e.g. those with the same level of income). For example, the idea that people with a similar ability to pay taxes should pay the same or similar amounts. Vertical equity relates to the fair treatment of people whose circumstances differ (e.g. those with different incomes). For example, the idea that people with a greater ability to pay taxes should pay more.

The equity-efficiency trade off

It is important to note that **equity** is *not* the same thing as **equality**, although market systems do produce great inequality of income and many people find the degree of inequality created to be unfair.

Such inequality can be useful in creating **incentives**. For example, the incentive to work relies on the fact that those in work have higher incomes than those not in work. The high incomes of those with high skill levels create an incentive for people to acquire skills. The incentive of high levels of profit is necessary to encourage entrepreneurs to accept risk.

Thus it is possible that measures that reduce inequality may enhance equity but also blunt economic incentives and cause inefficiency. The equity-efficiency trade off can be a useful evaluative concept for A2 students.

Chapter

3

Unit 3: **Introductory concepts** → Markets generally work well → Sometimes markets fail → This may justify government intervention → Government failure sometimes occurs

Profit and the Objectives of the Firm

Profit

Profit can be defined as total revenue (TR) minus total cost (TC): **Profit = TR – TC**. It is the reward (factor payment) to enterprise. This is the skill involved in spotting gaps in the market, organising other factors to produce output and taking risk.

Normal profit

Remember that economists measure a firm's cost of production as the **opportunity cost** of the factors of production used. Some factors (such as the owner's labour, unless they take a wage) may not be paid for but should be included in a full measure of costs.

Normal profit occurs when **TR = TC** and just enough revenue is generated to cover the money costs of production and the opportunity cost of the factors of production that have not been paid for (the money they could have generated in their next best use).

Normal profit is an economic profit of zero. Although the firm is making a money profit, this is no greater than could have been made had the factors used been employed in their next best use. In the long run, the firm must make at least normal profit or it will close, releasing factors of production to be used elsewhere.

Supernormal profit

Supernormal (or **monopoly** or **abnormal**) **profit** is an economic profit greater than zero, with **TR > TC**. The factors used by the firm generate more revenue than they could in any other use.

Profit maximisation

Economic theory traditionally assumes **rational, maximising behaviour** on the part of economic agents. Firms are assumed to maximise profits.

Profit maximisation occurs when **MC = MR**. The explanation of this is examined in Figure 3.1. At output level Q1, MR exceeds MC and the firm could increase profit by increasing output by one additional unit. At output level Q2, MC exceeds MR and the firm could increase profit by reducing output by one unit. If these two statements are correct then the profit maximising rule MC = MR must be true.

Figure 3.1: Profit maximisation

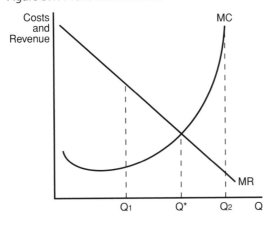

The functions of profit

Profit plays the following key economic roles:

1. **Rewarding entrepreneurs** for their role in combining factors of production, spotting gaps in the market and taking risks. Entrepreneurs play a key role in innovation and therefore in creating **dynamic efficiency** in the economy. This would not be possible without profit acting as an **incentive**.

2. **Allocating resources.** The **price mechanism** relies on the rationing, signalling and incentive functions to allocate resources to where they generate the most utility. When demand for a product rises, its relative price increases. As well as **signalling** a shortage of the product, this also boosts profit margins on each unit of the good produced, providing an **incentive** to firms to increase production. Thus efficient resource allocation in a market economy depends heavily on profit.

3. **An incentive to reduce/eliminate waste.** Waste (**x-inefficiency**) increases the costs of firms and reduces their profits. This can be illustrated using Figure 2.2 in Chapter 2.

4. **Profit is both an incentive to firms to invest and an important source of finance for that investment.** While much investment is financed through borrowing, a key source of finance is profits retained by firms in preference to distributing them in the form of dividends to shareholders. Governments are keen to encourage investment because it is an important source of economic growth, so it is common for them to offer **tax relief** on profits that are retained for investment purposes.

The divorce of ownership and control

The divorce of ownership and control refers to a situation where the owners of a firm are not involved in its day-to-day running and therefore cannot control its conduct. This may cause the firm to be run in a way that does not maximise profits because those who control the running of the firm (such as directors, managers and workers) may have different objectives and incentives from those who own it.

The divorce of ownership and control becomes increasingly apparent as a firm grows. There are four types of company:

| Sole trader | Partnership | | Private Limited Company | Public Limited Company |

Sole traders and partners own the company and run it on a day-to-day basis

Limited companies are owned by shareholders. In the case of a public limited company, shares can be traded on the stock market, thus the composition of ownership can change constantly. Shareholders appoint directors to run the firm and the divorce of ownership and control is apparent.

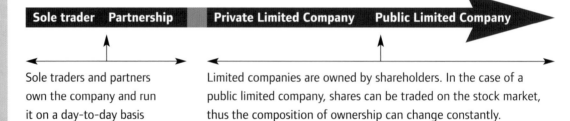

Profit is both an incentive to firms to invest and an important source of finance for investment.

Revenue maximisation	Some firms may wish to increase their market share in an industry and grow in size. This may allow them to attain **economies of scale** or to gain some form of **monopoly power**. This objective may also be driven by the management of the company whose salaries may be linked to the size of the firm in relation to others in the industry or its sales revenue. Revenue maximisation occurs when MR is equal to zero and is shown in Figure 3.2, at output Q2. The profit maximising level of output is Q1; by expanding output to Q2 the firm is reducing its profit, but increasing its sales revenue.
Sales maximisation (subject to the constraint of making at least normal profit)	A firm would maximise its total sales and make normal profit at Q3. This is where price (AR) = ATC. At this point total revenue equals total cost. If the firm expanded output any further it would make a loss and would go out of business in the long run. This objective may be driven by the same factors as revenue maximisation.

Figure 3.2: Alternative objectives of firms

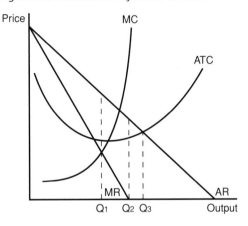

Satisficing	This describes a situation where a firm is run in such a way as to satisfy a key **stakeholder** (a stakeholder is anyone with an interest in the business and the way it is run – this includes shareholders, directors, managers, workers, customers and the local community).
	One form of satisficing is where those in control of the company seek to make sufficient profit to keep shareholders content, but pursue their own objectives subject to this constraint.
	Other forms of satisficing include not raising prices in order to prevent an investigation by the Competition Commission or to appease customers, even if raising the price would increase profit. Equally, the firm may reward workers with higher wages in order to prevent industrial action.
Evaluation: The effects of the divorce of ownership and control	Divorce of ownership and control may affect the **conduct** of the firm (whether it pursues profit maximisation or some other objective) and its **performance** (in terms of economic efficiency and equity).
	The extent to which divorce of ownership and control affects a firm's conduct depends on a number of factors, including:

- How accountable the directors and management of the firm are to shareholders. Shareholders can remove directors at the company's Annual General Meeting (AGM), but may lack the information required to judge whether the company is maximising profits.

- Whether incentives are in place to encourage directors and staff to profit maximise. This might be achieved through profit-related pay or by encouraging employees to be shareholders (perhaps by making shares available to them at less than the market price).

- How large the firm is. The larger the firm, the more difficult it may be to exercise control over those responsible for its running.

The divorce of ownership and control is often thought to affect the firm's performance in an adverse manner. Revenue maximisation (Q2 in Figure 3.2) and sales maximisation (Q3) both result in the firm producing additional units beyond the point where P = MC (the condition for allocative efficiency, shown by the point where AR crosses the MC curve). The resources used to generate these extra units could have generated more utility elsewhere and a **misallocation of resources** has occurred.

However, the divorce of ownership and control may prevent the firm being too **short termist** in its outlook. Shareholders tend to want high profits as quickly as possible and this may mean that the firm sacrifices its future performance in order to pay high dividends at the current time. It may, for example, under invest because of the demands of shareholders for high levels of profit and dividends. This may prevent the firm from growing and performing efficiently in the future. It is possible that those running a company may take a longer term view than shareholders would do.

A further problem is that short termism can jeopardise safety, especially in industries such as air and railway travel and the provision of utilities such as gas and electricity. Maintaining infrastructure and putting in place adequate procedures to ensure safety may be costly and serve to reduce profit below its maximum level. In this case, it may be helpful for performance if the conduct of the firm is not driven by shareholders, but instead by those responsible for the day-to-day management of the firm or by government regulators.

It is also possible that the divorce of ownership and control might produce more **equitable** outcomes, although this is a matter of value judgements and belongs to the field of **normative** economics. Profit maximisation may put unreasonable stresses on staff as they strive to bear down on costs, for example, while satisficing behaviour may avoid this pressure.

'Not for profit' organisations

A 'not for profit' organisation (NPO) does not distribute profit to shareholders, but exists to provide services that are of **public benefit**. Examples include charities, trade unions and public arts organisations. Network Rail is an NPO. It owns and operates Britain's rail infrastructure and states its aim as follows: "We strive to provide Britain with a safe, reliable and efficient railway fit for the 21st century".

<table>
<tr><td>Chapter
4</td><td>Unit 3: Introductory concepts → Markets generally work well → Sometimes markets fail
→ This may justify government intervention → Government failure sometimes occurs

Competitive Markets</td></tr>
</table>

This box is repeated at the start of each chapter on the structure-conduct-performance model (traditional theory of the firm). You are recommended to read it each time.

0% ————→ INCREASING MARKET CONCENTRATION ————→ 100%

Perfect Competition　　　Monopolistic Competition　　　Oligopoly　　　Monopoly

A market is concentrated if a small number of firms hold a large market share. Market *structure* refers to concentration; the height of any entry barriers; whether firms sell homogeneous products and the knowledge firms and consumers possess.

Market structure impacts on the *conduct* of firms (e.g. do they set their own prices or accept the market price? Do they compete on non-price factors? Do they collude with other firms?).

The conduct of firms has implications for the economic *performance* of the market in terms of efficient resource allocation, productive efficiency and possibly equity considerations too.

Contestable markets theory contrasts with traditional theory. It stresses how the threat of new competition affects conduct and performance rather than the level of existing competition.

Structure

Perfectly competitive markets have the following characteristics:

1. Many buyers and many sellers – 0% concentration.

2. Homogeneous products – each firm's product is identical.

3. Perfect information – each firm and consumer has perfect knowledge of market conditions, such as the price charged by every firm in the market.

4. There are no entry or exit barriers – so there is complete freedom of entry and exit to and from the market.

Conduct

● It is assumed that firms are profit maximisers and produce a level of output such that MC = MR.

● All firms accept the ruling market price and are therefore **price takers**. Because the products of each firm are homogeneous, they are perfect substitutes for each other. The perfect knowledge assumed of the firm's customers ensures that they would switch to other sellers if the firm charged more than the going rate. The firm faces a **perfectly elastic demand curve** (see Chapter 1 to understand how this affects average and marginal revenue).

● No consumer buys enough of the market output to have the power to lower prices. There is no **monopsony** power (see Chapter 5).

● There is no branding or non-price competition of any kind.

Although perfect competition may not exist in the real world, there are still markets that can be considered to be highly competitive. Good examples of competitive markets include book retailing, clothing, computer hardware, home and car insurance, opticians and parcel delivery.

Performance evaluation

Allocative efficiency – a positive concept. For the price mechanism to allocate resources efficiently (revise the rationing, signalling and incentive functions of prices from the AS level version of this revision guide), markets must be perfectly competitive. This is because the price mechanism only works properly through the reaction of consumers and firms to changes in relative prices (all market participants are price takers). Also, consumers can only make utility maximising decisions if they have perfect knowledge.

Further, the **incentive function** of prices relies on supernormal profit attracting new entrants into the market (which in turn requires freedom of entry, as in perfect competition). Remember that supernormal profit is profit in excess of that needed to keep the factors of production in their present use; total revenue exceeds the opportunity cost of the factors used.

The incentive function is illustrated in Figures 4.1 and 4.2. In Figure 4.1, high demand for the product has generated a supernormal profit. This is a short run equilibrium. Note that the price is set by industry supply and demand and accepted by the firm. For the firm shown in the diagram, the profit maximising output is at Q where MC = MR. This output generates a **total revenue** (P x Q) equal to 0PaQ. The **total cost** of producing this output can be calculated by multiplying the average cost of a unit of output (bQ) and the output produced. Total costs will therefore be equal to 0cbQ. Since the total revenue exceeds total cost the firm is making **supernormal profits** equal to Pabc, which can also be stated as (average revenue – average cost) multiplied by output Q. Normal profit is already included in the average cost curve.

Figure 4.1: Short run supernormal profit

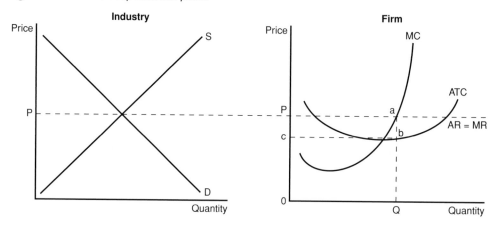

Figure 4.2: The role of profit in the incentive function

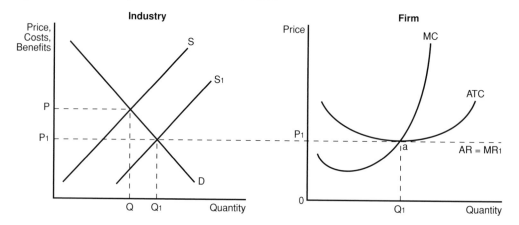

The supernormal profit generated by the high demand now provides an incentive for new firms to enter the market. In Figure 4.2, the entry of new firms into the market causes the industry supply curve to shift right (from S to S1). The result is that more resources (Q to Q1) are now allocated to making the product. Resources have followed consumer demand and are being used where they generate most utility. For confirmation that the outcome is allocatively efficient, check that **P = MC** on the right-hand side of the diagram.

In the event that there was low demand for a product, firms would make a short run economic loss and some would leave the industry. Again, this helps resource allocation to adjust to consumer demand.

Long run equilibrium under perfect competition is defined by normal profit (**AR = AC**) and meeting the condition for allocative efficiency in the absence of externalities, namely P = MC.

Productive efficiency – a positive concept. In a highly competitive market where firms are price takers, any firm failing to achieve minimum average cost would suffer economic losses. This would cause the firm to leave the market in the long run, releasing the resources used to be allocated elsewhere. Each firm achieves the lowest possible average cost when the market is in long run equilibrium.

It is assumed in the standard theory of the firm that firms produce on their AC curve (with the profit motive providing an incentive to eliminate waste). This assumption is most realistic in highly competitive markets where firms suffering from **x-inefficiency** would be unlikely to survive.

Dynamic efficiency – a positive concept. It is sometimes argued that perfect competition may not be dynamically efficient. The lack of any long run supernormal profit may prevent firms from financing research and development for example, while complete freedom of market entry might discourage firms from innovating (other firms could simply copy the innovation). In reality, however, some markets that are highly competitive, without being perfectly so, may exhibit some innovation, especially if it is possible to patent or copyright those innovations in order to gain a competitive edge over rivals.

Equity considerations – a normative concept. In a world of highly competitive markets, no firm would make the huge supernormal profits that are achievable in some concentrated market structures. It might also be considered fair that in competitive markets consumers pay a price that accurately reflects the costs of producing goods. In highly competitive labour markets, the huge wage inequalities that some people find distasteful would not be present. As explained already, however, these possible gains in equity might come at the expense of blunting the dynamic performance of the economy. This is a possible example of the **equity-efficiency trade-off**.

Shut-down points

A firm will leave a competitive market in the long run if it does not make at least normal profit (because this implies that the factors of production used can generate more revenue elsewhere).

In the short run, however, a loss making firm may continue in business. This is because the firm is already committed to paying its fixed costs even if no output is produced. If it can command a price greater than the average variable cost of production, each unit sold will make some contribution to paying the fixed costs and therefore reduce overall losses. If the firm cannot even cover its variable costs, it will shut down immediately.

Chapter

5

Unit 3: Introductory concepts → Markets generally work well → **Sometimes markets fail** → This may justify government intervention → Government failure sometimes occurs

Monopoly and Monopsony

This box is repeated at the start of each chapter on the structure-conduct-performance model (traditional theory of the firm). You are recommended to read it each time.

0% ──────────────→ **INCREASING MARKET CONCENTRATION** ──────────→ **100%**

Perfect Competition   Monopolistic Competition   Oligopoly   Monopoly

A market is concentrated if a small number of firms hold a large market share. Market *structure* refers to concentration; the height of any entry barriers; whether firms sell homogeneous products and the knowledge firms and consumers possess.

Market structure impacts on the *conduct* of firms (e.g. do they set their own prices or accept the market price? Do they compete on non-price factors? Do they collude with other firms?)

The conduct of firms has implications for the economic *performance* of the market in terms of efficient resource allocation, productive efficiency and possibly equity considerations too.

Contestable markets theory contrasts with traditional theory. It stresses how the threat of new competition affects conduct and performance rather than the level of existing competition.

Structure

1. A single supplier – market concentration is 100%.

2. Entry barriers high enough to prevent new market entry.

Conduct

● Monopoly firms enjoy **price making power** (see Chapter 1 for the effects of this power on average and marginal revenue). There are no substitutes for the product and thus the monopolist is likely to face an **inelastic demand curve**, allowing the freedom to raise prices while suffering a less than proportionate contraction of demand for the product. **Total revenue** (TR = P x Q) rises as a result, as does profit.

● In order to raise price the monopolist must restrict the quantity supplied. The monopolist is said to be **constrained by the demand curve**: a monopolist can choose its price or output, but not both.

Performance evaluation: (1) The case against monopoly

There is no distinction between short and long run equilibrium in the model of pure monopoly. Short run supernormal profits can be sustained into the long run due to high entry barriers. Figure 5.1 shows the monopoly equilibrium position. The profit-maximising level of output is at Q and the firm will charge price P. This will generate total revenue equal to 0PaQ, but the cost of producing this output will be 0cbQ. As total revenue exceeds total costs the firm will generate supernormal profits equal to Pabc.

Figure 5.1: Monopoly equilibrium

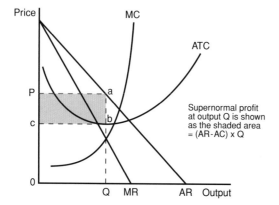

The supernormal profit enjoyed by the monopolist has been accompanied by a market failure: At Q, consumers value additional units of output at a higher price (P) than the opportunity cost of making them (MC). The monopolist is extracting a price from consumers that is above the cost of resources used in making the product. The needs and wants of consumers are not being satisfied as the product is being **under consumed**. The result is **allocative inefficiency**. Note further that, by restricting quantity, the monopolist voluntarily foregoes some economies of scale, so **productive efficiency** (producing at minimum AC) is not achieved.

The damage done by the misallocation of resources is illustrated in Figure 5.2, which assumes constant marginal and average costs for simplicity.

A perfectly competitive industry will produce in the long run where market demand (AR) = market supply (AC = MC). The equilibrium output and price is at Qc and Pc. At this point, P = MC and the industry is allocatively efficient. As the monopolist profit maximises (MR = MC) and restricts quantity (Qm) the price rises from Pc to Pm. The concept of **consumer surplus** is central here (the gap between the price a consumer has to pay and the maximum price that they would have been willing to pay). The price rise transfers some of the consumer surplus, on the Qm units that are still sold, to the monopolist as supernormal profit. Meanwhile, the consumer surplus that would have been enjoyed on Qc-Qm units under competitive conditions is lost altogether. This is known as a **deadweight welfare loss**.

Figure 5.2: Comparing monopoly and competition

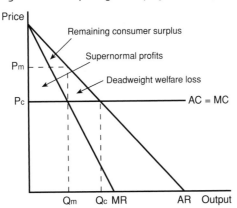

Firms operating under monopoly conditions may become lazy due to a lack of competitive pressure and allow some waste in the production process, leading to technical or **x-inefficiency**. This can be linked to the divorce of ownership and control: unless shareholders are very effective at holding the directors and managers of the firm to account, such x-inefficiency can persist.

Equity

Monopoly can be argued to contribute to unfair outcomes in the following ways:

● The consumer is faced by a lack of choice.

● The monopolist is seen to use their price making powers at the expense of the consumer (exploitation?). Huge profits of corporations with monopoly power can be seen as contributing to unfair distributions of income.

Performance evaluation: (2) Defending monopoly

The following arguments can be used to highlight the benefits that a monopoly might bring to a market:

● The comparison of monopoly and perfect competition in Figure 5.2 ignored the fact that monopolies may achieve large **economies of scale**. This may allow a monopolist to produce at a lower price and a higher output than a perfectly competitive industry.

● It is often argued that monopolies contribute to the **dynamic efficiency** of the economy, because monopoly profits may help fund research and development, leading to innovation. Against this, it may be that a lack of competition may reduce the incentive to innovate.

● Firms seeking monopoly power may act in socially useful ways, for example sponsoring community events to foster **customer loyalty**. Advertising revenue from large firms helps pay for services such as ITV that are provided free of charge to the consumer.

● Some very powerful large firms operate an alternative model of selling at a low price in high quantities (Tesco and ToysR Us, for example). The implications for resource allocation are much more favourable.

Equity

The outcome of those monopolies that work on a low price model may seem more efficient and also fairer than traditional monopoly outcomes, although this low price model may help drive competitors out of business and restrict choice (leading to the creation of what some have dubbed 'Tescotowns').

Monopoly power

While there are some **pure monopolies** (such as regional water firms) these are few in number, and even powerful firms such as Microsoft do not enjoy 100% market share. As a result the **working definition** of a monopoly is a firm that enjoys a 25% market share, because this is often large enough for it to have a substantial influence on market prices.

Monopoly power should probably be understood as **price making power**: the ability of a firm to set its own prices rather than be dictated to by market conditions. Factors contributing to monopoly power include:

● **High market concentration.**

● **Product differentiation.** Where a firm has been able physically to differentiate its product or to create desirable image characteristics (branding) this helps create consumer loyalty, and reduce the price elasticity of demand. Branded clothing is a good example.

● **Consumer inertia.** In markets including utilities such as gas and electricity, consumers are often reluctant to switch providers because of the perceived time and effort involved. Again this reduces the elasticity of demand.

● **Imperfect knowledge** can result in firms being able to charge customers high prices, if those customers do not know they can do better elsewhere. Again, utilities may be an example. It can be difficult for customers to gain the information needed for price comparisons, although price comparison websites such as Uswitch are making this easier.

● **High entry barriers** contribute to price making power by reducing the possibility of new entry in the event that a firm makes supernormal profit.

The growth of firms and development of monopolies

Firms can grow **externally** through mergers and takeovers. Motivations for external growth include the desire to acquire greater market share and therefore power. This may allow firms to achieve economies of scale, to acquire valuable brand names owned by other firms or to gain greater control over the supply chain. Firms can also grow **internally** by expanding their operations and perhaps diversifying into new products.

The ways in which monopolies can develop are summarised in the following table:

Horizontal integration	Where two firms join at the same stage of production in the same industry. For example two car manufacturers merge, or a leading bank successfully takes over another bank. The ITV network is now a monopoly because regional companies merged in search of economies of scale.
Vertical integration	Where a firm develops market power by integrating with the different stages of production in an industry e.g. by buying its suppliers or controlling the main retail outlets. A good example is the oil industry where many of the leading companies are both producers and refiners of crude oil.

Figure 5.3: Price discrimination

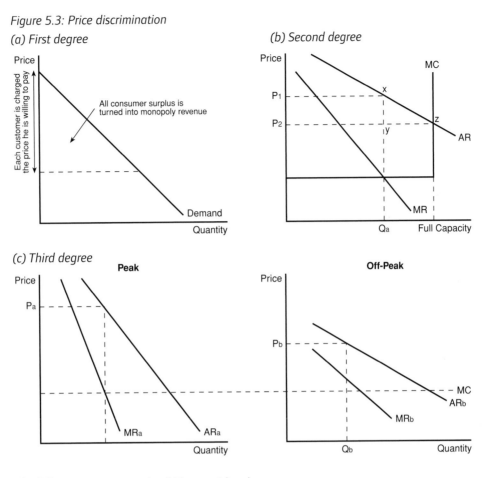

(a) First degree

(b) Second degree

(c) Third degree

Evaluation:
Is price discrimination in the interest of the consumer?

The following arguments should be considered:

● **Consumer surplus** is reduced in most cases – representing a loss of consumer welfare. However some consumers who can buy the product at a lower price may benefit. Previously they may have been excluded from consuming the good.

● In most cases price is greater than marginal cost and therefore firms are not achieving **allocative efficiency**.

● Price discrimination is clearly in the interests of firms who achieve higher profits.

● The profits made in one market may allow firms to **cross-subsidise** loss making activities/services that have important **social benefits**. For example, profits made on commuter services may allow railway companies to support loss making rural or night time services.

Monopsony

A monopsony exists when there is a sole buyer of a product. Monopsony power exists when a firm buys a large enough proportion of market output to be able to drive down prices. Large supermarkets may be able to drive down the prices they pay their suppliers, for example. For a discussion of monopsony in the labour market, see Chapter 14.

Where monopsony power is strong, it is unlikely that supplying firms can make more than **normal profit**. Thus monopsony power can be advantageous in countering any monopoly power that might be present on the supply side of the market. **Resource allocation** is likely to be more efficient when prices are lower and driven down to normal profit levels.

On occasion, however, monopsony power can threaten the viability of supplying businesses. Many farmers, for example, claim to be unable to supply milk profitably at the prices that supermarkets are willing to pay. There are **equity** considerations here and a need to take into account the social benefits that may be offered by the agricultural sector.

Chapter

6

Unit 3: Introductory concepts → **Markets generally work well** → Sometimes markets fail → This may justify government intervention → Government failure sometimes occurs

Monopolistic Competition

> **This box is repeated at the start of each chapter on the structure-conduct-performance model (traditional theory of the firm). You are recommended to read it each time.**
>
> **0%** ——————————→ **INCREASING MARKET CONCENTRATION** ——————————→ **100%**
>
> Perfect Competition   Monopolistic Competition   Oligopoly   Monopoly
>
> A market is concentrated if a small number of firms hold a large market share. Market *structure* refers to concentration; the height of any entry barriers; whether firms sell homogeneous products and the knowledge firms and consumers possess.
>
> Market structure impacts on the *conduct* of firms (e.g. do they set their own prices or accept the market price? Do they compete on non-price factors? Do they collude with other firms?).
>
> The conduct of firms has implications for the economic *performance* of the market in terms of efficient resource allocation, productive efficiency and possibly equity considerations too.
>
> Contestable markets theory contrasts with traditional theory. It stresses how the threat of new competition affects conduct and performance rather than the level of existing competition.

Structure

1. Monopolistic competition has all the characteristics of perfect competition – many buyers and sellers, perfect information and the absence of entry barriers **except products may be slightly differentiated**.

Examples of monopolistically competitive markets may include regional markets for services, such as the market for plumbers, electricians and hairdressers.

Conduct

● The scope for **product differentiation** allows for the possibility that firms may attempt 'moderate branding' of their product or service through advertising and image creation.

● Firms have some small degree of **price making power** due to product differentiation. **Consumer loyalty** allows them to raise their price while retaining some of their customers. Firms will face a downward sloping demand curve.

Performance evaluation

Figure 6.1: Short run supernormal profit

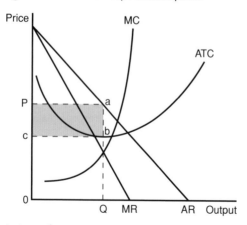

As in perfect competition it is possible for a firm to make either supernormal profit or an economic loss in the short run. In Figure 6.1 the firm is shown to make a **supernormal profit**. The profit maximising level of output is at Q and the firm will charge price P. This will generate total revenue equal to 0PaQ, but the cost of producing this output will be 0cbQ. As total revenue exceeds total costs the firm will generate supernormal profits equal to Pabc.

The diagram is essentially the same as the monopoly equilibrium diagram. It should be noted, however, that demand might be rather more elastic than under monopoly because of the presence of good (if slightly differentiated) **substitutes** under monopolistic competition.

As under conditions of perfect competition, this supernormal profit cannot persist in the long run. The lack of entry barriers allows firms to respond to the incentive offered by supernormal profit and enter the market. As new firms enter, the supernormal profit is eroded away as the demand curve facing each firm shifts to the left. Long run equilibrium under monopolistic competition is thus defined by normal profit. This is illustrated in Figure 6.2

Figure 6.2: Long run equilibrium under monopolistic competition

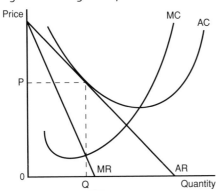

This diagram is particularly difficult to draw accurately. The following strategy is recommended:
- Draw the AC curve
- Draw the AR curve such that there is a point of tangency with the AC curve.
- Draw the MR curve to be twice as steep as the AR curve.
- Draw the MC curve. This must cut the MR curve directly below the point of tangency between AR and AC **and** must go through the bottom point of the AC curve.
- Finally, draw dotted lines for the price and quantity coordinates. Quantity is established where MR=MC, reading up to the demand curve to show the price.

The outcome is not as efficient as if the market had been perfectly competitive. The mild product differentiation results in a higher price, which is now raised above the marginal cost (**allocative inefficiency**). Remember that the price indicates marginal benefit, so we now have MB > MC and there are additional units of the good that could have been produced, which would have brought a net benefit.

To raise the price, firms have also had to restrict quantity and voluntarily forego some economies of scale, so **productive efficiency** (lowest possible AC) is not achieved.

However, this market structure is much more efficient than a monopoly and would generally still be regarded as functioning well. Under monopoly, the price would be much higher, the contraction of demand greater and thus the **misallocation of resources** more serious.

Monopolistically competitive markets may not be favourable for the **dynamic efficiency** of the economy. While the possibility of gaining an edge over rivals is attractive, this is unlikely to be sufficient to act as a significant incentive to innovate due to the lack of entry barriers. The lack of supernormal profit could also possibly leave firms short of investment funds.

Equity

Consumer choice in this type of market is good and firms might offer excellent service as they attempt to differentiate themselves from competitors. The issue of consumer exploitation is not as strong a concern as under monopoly.

Chapter

7

Unit 3: Introductory concepts → Markets generally work well → **Sometimes markets fail** → This may justify government intervention → Government failure sometimes occurs

Oligopoly

> **This box is repeated at the start of each chapter on the structure-conduct-performance model (traditional theory of the firm). You are recommended to read it each time.**
>
> 0% ———————→ INCREASING MARKET CONCENTRATION ———————→ 100%
>
> Perfect Competition   Monopolistic Competition   Oligopoly   Monopoly
>
> A market is concentrated if a small number of firms hold a large market share. Market *structure* refers to concentration; the height of any entry barriers; whether firms sell homogeneous products and the knowledge firms and consumers possess.
>
> Market structure impacts on the *conduct* of firms (e.g. do they set their own prices or accept the market price? Do they compete on non-price factors? Do they collude with other firms?).
>
> The conduct of firms has implications for the economic *performance* of the market in terms of efficient resource allocation, productive efficiency and possibly equity considerations too.
>
> Contestable markets theory contrasts with traditional theory. It stresses how the threat of new competition affects conduct and performance rather than the level of existing competition.

Structure

1. An oligopoly is a concentrated market dominated by a few producers (measured by the 'x' firm **concentration ratio**, the combined market share of the largest 'x' firms). There may be smaller firms on the periphery of the market.

2. Firms offer differentiated products.

3. Entry barriers are usually present and vary in size from one oligopoly to another.

Examples of oligopolies include: Electricity generation, petrol retail and production, telecommunications, digital television and washing powder.

Conduct

The concentrated nature of oligopolistic markets ensures that firms are **interdependent**. There is no uniquely defined best strategy for a firm to follow because the outcome of any strategy depends on the actions and reactions of rivals.

Thus the pricing and output decisions of oligopolists depend on the **strategies** that they choose to adopt in the face of interdependence.

Collusive oligopoly occurs when firms refrain from competition, especially on price, and act as if they were one firm: a joint monopoly. Collusion tends to produce the high price, low quantity outcomes that are typical of monopoly. Collusion can be undertaken **formally** (overtly), for example through a **cartel**, where firms agree a price and a fixed quota of output for each firm. It can also be **implicit** (tacit), where firms do not reach an agreement with one another but simply come to recognise that it is not in any firm's interests to spark a price war. Some oligopolies exhibit **price leadership**, where a major player in the market sets the price and other firms follow.

Competitive oligopoly occurs when firms compete on price. Periodic price wars break out in some oligopolistic markets, and the nature of interdependence makes them difficult to bring to an end because no firm wants to be the first to fail to respond to a rival's price cut. Prices under competitive oligopoly tend to be driven to lower levels, while output is higher.

To compete or collude?

Factors favouring collusive oligopoly:	**Factors favouring competitive oligopoly:**

- Small number of firms.
- Firms have similar costs.
- High entry barriers.
- If the effect of any cheating on market price is not easily detected and punished.
- Ineffective competition policy.
- Consumer loyalty – making the gains from price competition less attractive.
- Consumer inertia – as above.

- More firms (a less concentrated oligopoly).
- New market entry.
- One firm has significant cost advantages.
- Firms produce homogenous products.
- A saturated market, where firms can only grow by taking market share from rivals.

In general, a relatively stable market may foster collusion. Anything disturbing that stability or giving even one firm a reason to try to undercut rivals is likely to cause price competition.

Performance evaluation

With regard to both efficiency and equity, the outcome of oligopoly depends heavily on whether firms operate in a collusive or competitive fashion.

Collusion produces:

- Higher prices.
- Lower output.
- Allocative inefficiency – as prices are greater than marginal cost.

Thus collusive monopoly produces **market failure**. Refer to Chapter 5 for more detail. For collusive oligopoly, it can be useful to draw Figure 5.2 that shows the deadweight welfare loss from monopoly compared to perfect competition. Collusive oligopoly also produces **equity** concerns regarding consumer exploitation.

Cheating on a cartel agreement can be explained by the "Prisoners' Dilemma".

Competitive oligopoly produces more efficient and, arguably, more equitable outcomes. It seems that such markets work fairly well. Additionally, it is useful to note that product differentiation under oligopoly may offer consumers significant choice.

Illustrating inter-dependence: (1) The kinked demand curve

One of the best known illustrations of **interdependence** under oligopoly is the kinked demand curve. This can be used to explain long periods of price stability under oligopoly. It can also be used to explain why price wars periodically break out and are difficult to bring to an end.

The theory of kinked demand makes two key **assumptions**:

● When one firm raises its price other firms do not follow suit. The firm raising its price thus faces a more than proportionate contraction in demand (elastic response). See the section of the demand curve above price P in Figure 7.1.

● When one firm cuts its price other firms do likewise. No market share is gained from rivals, although the overall market may expand a little. Demand extends less than proportionately (inelastic response). See the section of the demand curve below price P in Figure 7.1.

Given these assumptions it is likely that the industry will see a period of price stability. This is because any firm that changes its price will see its total revenue and profits fall.

If the industry is operating at price P in Figure 7.1, any firm that raises its prices whilst facing an elastic demand curve will see its total revenue and profits fall. Similarly, any firm cutting its price whilst facing an inelastic demand curve will experience a similar fall in revenue and profit.

Note how this illustrates interdependence; the model makes assumptions about how rivals will react to price changes. This assumption may or may not be accurate in any given oligopolistic market.

Figure 7.1: The theory of kinked demand (illustrating interdependence)

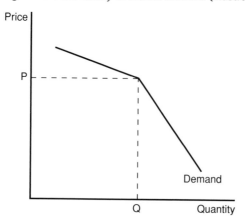

Illustrating inter-dependence: (2) A duopoly cartel

Cartel agreements can be very difficult to sustain. Because they are usually illegal, they cannot be enforced in the courts. Any firm breaking a cartel agreement in isolation (for example, by producing more than an agreed quota of output) stands to gain substantially from doing so. The **joint monopoly** formed by the cartel means that, for each individual firm, marginal revenue is greater than marginal cost. It is therefore possible to increase profits by producing more output, as long as other firms do not also cheat on the agreement.

Again, **interdependence** is apparent: The outcome for any single firm of cheating on a cartel agreement depends on whether other firms also cheat.

The incentive to cheat on a cartel agreement can be further explained by the following analysis. The scenario is popularly known as the **Prisoners' Dilemma** and is an example of **game theory**.

Suppose two firms in a duopoly cartel will make the profits shown in the matrix, depending on their decision as to whether to cheat on the agreement by producing more output or to collude by sticking to their quotas.

Profits for Firm A are shown first in each case		**Firm A**	
		Cheat	Collude
Firm B	Cheat	Zero, Zero	-£2m, £20m
	Collude	£20m, -£2m	£12m, £12m

The best collective outcome for the two firms is to sustain the collusive agreement, allowing them to make a joint profit of £24 million. However, individually the **dominant strategy** is to cheat. Consider the column of the table where Firm A cheats. Firm A will make a supernormal profit of £20m while firm B will make a loss of £2m. However, if Firm B also cheats it will make a normal profit, which is preferable to a loss of £2m by sticking to the agreement. Clearly when both firms cheat, and make only normal profits, they are in a worse situation than if they had colluded and made £12m profit.

The cartel is therefore under enormous pressure to break up although the table earlier in this chapter explains some circumstances in which it may be sustained.

Illustrating inter-dependence (3) First mover advantage

The order in which firms enter a market can have a substantial effect on the outcome. The first mover is the first significant entrant into a market. Whether to be the first mover in a market is a strategic decision for a firm and its outcome may depend partly on the actions and reactions of rivals. Therefore, it helps to illustrate **interdependence** and belongs to the field of game theory.

In the market for MP3 players, Apple is often considered to have been a first mover with its iPod. Although not the first entrant, Apple was the most significant early entrant.

First mover advantages	First mover disadvantages
• Establish reputation and earn brand loyalty.	• Free rider effects. Second movers can copy the technology created by the first mover (unless patent protected).
• Customers may face costs if they later wish to switch from first mover (e.g. songs purchased on Apples iTunes may not be transferable to non-iPod MP3 players).	• Risk. First movers do not have full information about consumer appetite for the product.
• First movers may take control of scarce resources.	• Late movers have more time to assess technological changes and/or customer mood.

Chapter

8

Unit 3: Introductory concepts → **Markets generally work well** → Sometimes markets fail
→ This may justify government intervention → Government failure sometimes occurs

Contestable Markets

The threat of new entry	The theory of contestable markets is a modern development that considers how the threat of new entry might affect the conduct of **incumbent firms** (those already in the market). Potential competition is seen as a key influence on firms, rather than just actual competition (the current degree of market concentration).
Contestable markets	A contestable market is one that is open to new entrants. It has the following features: 1. Low entry and exit barriers, particularly **sunk costs**. Sunk costs are costs that are not recoverable on leaving the market. Many of these are start up costs, such as capital equipment and advertising. 2. The potential for post-entry supernormal profit for new firms. A market with no entry or exit barriers is regarded as **perfectly contestable**. Thus markets exhibiting the characteristics of perfect or monopolistic competition are perfectly contestable. But a monopoly could, in theory, be perfectly contestable too, if there was a single firm but an absence of entry and exit barriers. Competition and contestability are two different things!
Barriers to entry	To understand whether a market is contestable, it is vital to have a good understanding of the factors that can act as barriers to entry (making it more difficult for new firms to enter a market). Some key barriers to entry are summarised in the table:

Patents	These give a firm the legal protection to produce a patented product for a number of years. Patents are government enforced intellectual property rights to prevent the entry of rivals. They are generally assigned for 17-20 years and give the owner an exclusive right to prevent others from using their products, ideas, inventions or processes. A good example of this is the patent on the Dyson vacuum cleaner.
Vertical integration	Control over supplies and distribution can be very important. For example, many major international oil companies are fully vertically integrated. They control oil extraction, refining and retail outlets to maintain their market power.
Limit pricing	Firms may adopt predatory pricing policies by lowering prices to a level that would force any new entrants to operate at a loss.
Absolute cost advantages	Lower costs, perhaps due to being in the market for some time, allow the existing monopolist to cut prices and win price wars.
Advertising	High levels of advertising enable firms to establish branded products and win customer loyalty. New entrants into the market must therefore spend substantial amounts on advertising to compete, which could deter entry.
Sunk costs	Some industries have very high start-up costs or a high ratio of fixed to variable costs. Some of these costs might be unrecoverable if an entrant opts to leave the market. This acts as a disincentive to enter the industry.
International trade restrictions	Trade restrictions, such as tariffs and quotas, should also be considered as a barrier. Foreign rivals cannot compete with firms in a protected domestic market.

Factors enhancing contestability	Capital costs are often seen as sunk costs and can reduce contestability. However, where there is a thriving second hand market for capital equipment, start up costs are lowered and more of the outlay can be recouped if a firm decides to leave the market. As a result, second hand markets enhance contestabilty. A good example of where second hand markets have improved contestabilty is the bus industry.

Markets may also be more contestable when there are powerful firms in related markets who are able to diversify. For example, Virgin has been able to enter many markets that might not have been open to competition from less established names.

Government policy (**deregulation**) has made a number of industries more contestable in recent years, including the bus industry, directory enquiries and gas and electricity supply.

Conduct of firms in contestable markets

The crucial assumption of the theory of contestable markets is that the conduct of incumbent firms can be influenced by the threat of new entry into their market. If this assumption is correct, firms might be expected to behave in the following ways:

Entry limit pricing

In a market with low (or zero) entry barriers, supernormal profit is likely to attract new entry. If incumbent firms wish to prevent this, then it is necessary for them to price at a lower level than that which would create maximum profit in the short run. If there are no entry barriers at all, then entry limit pricing will entail pricing at the normal profit level, regardless of the current concentration of the market.

Figure 8.1 shows the traditional monopoly diagram, with profit maximisation where MR = MC at output Q1 and price P1. If there are no entry barriers present, the monopolist may instead be forced to price at the normal profit level, where AR = AC. Output and price would then be Q2 and P2 respectively.

Figure 8.1: Entry limit pricing where the market is perfectly contestable (no entry barriers at all)

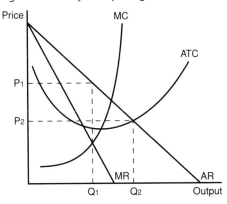

Where there are some entry barriers present, this permits firms to make some supernormal profit whilst still deterring new entry. How much supernormal profit they make will depend on the height of the entry barriers. Thus it is assumed that firms price in such a way as to make the highest level of profit compatible with deterring the entry of new firms into the industry.

Building artificial entry barriers

Firms operating in highly contestable markets may have an interest in making their market less contestable by building artificial entry barriers. This would then permit them to charge higher prices and make more profit without attracting new entry. Examples of artificial entry barriers can be found in the table earlier in this chapter, and include heavy advertising expenditure, product differentiation, investing in spare capacity and acquiring a reputation for predatory pricing. It should be noted, however, that some attempts to build artificial entry barriers might be seen as **restrictive practices** and may attract intervention from the **competition authorities**.

Hit and run competition

Highly contestable markets are not just easy to enter; they are also easy to leave. In such a market, it is possible for new firms to enter for brief periods of time and make a supernormal profit, even if they are then forced to leave the market quickly (e.g. by predatory action from incumbent firms).

Performance of contestable markets

The main insight of contestable markets theory is that a lack of entry barriers may force firms in **concentrated markets** to price at **competitive levels**. The performance outcomes under contestable markets are thus very similar to those for perfect competition.

Chapter

9

Unit 3: Introductory concepts → **Markets generally work well** → Sometimes markets fail → This may justify government intervention → Government failure sometimes occurs

Privatisation, Deregulation and Internal Markets

Reducing government intervention

Privatisation and deregulation are government policies aimed at increasing economic efficiency. However, they are not, as such, interventions in markets. Rather, they aim to reduce the role of government in markets and are inspired by the belief that competitive markets generally work well. This belief also leads governments to create internal markets.

Privatisation and deregulation have both macro and micro economic effects. From a macro perspective, they can be seen as supply side policies intended to promote economic growth.

Privatisation

Privatisation is the transfer of economic activity from the public sector (the state) to the private sector. Examples include:

1. The **sale of nationalised firms**. Firms that are owned by the state on behalf of the people can be sold into private hands through the issuing of shares. Many of today's utility providers were once state owned monopolies, including British Telecom and British Gas.

2. **Contracting out.** Many services provided by the state can be produced by private firms. For example, hospital and school cleaning services and the running of council leisure centres are contracted out to private firms. More recently, private firms such as BUPA have been paid to provide operations for NHS patients in order to reduce waiting lists.

3. **Competitive tendering.** When services are contracted out, firms usually have to bid ('tender') for the contract on the basis of price charged and/or quality of service provided.

4. The **sale of state owned assets**, such as the sale of council houses to their tenants.

5. The **Private Finance Initiative** (PFI), which is an example of a **Public Private Partnership** (PPP). The state has commissioned the private sector to pay for and build new schools, hospitals and prisons which are then leased on a long term basis to the state.

Economic circumstances sometimes create a need for **nationalisation**. For example, a financial crisis during 2007 and 2008 saw a number of banks taken wholly, or in part, into government ownership.

Evaluating privatisation

● Privatisation is inspired by the belief that private firms use resources more efficiently than the state sector does. The primary reason for this is the profit motive and, as a result, private firms will strive to reduce waste and **x-inefficiency**. However, private firms do produce some waste. This is especially likely for monopolies, or where there is a divorce of ownership and control and shareholders are ineffective in holding directors and managers to account.

Figure 9.1: X-inefficiency

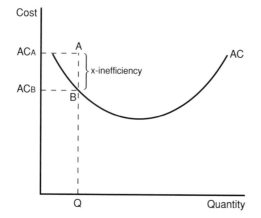

X-inefficiency is illustrated in Figure 9.1, where output Q is produced at average cost AC_A when it could be produced at a cost as low as AC_B.

- Privatisation may also help improve **resource allocation**. This is because private firms respond to market signals. However, some privatised firms have simply moved from being state monopolies to private monopolies, which may be more likely to charge higher prices and **exploit** the consumer. It may therefore be necessary to accompany privatisation by other measures such as **deregulation** to reduce entry barriers and make the market more **contestable**. Alternatively, it may be necessary for governments to regulate the prices charged as, for example, OFWAT does in the water industry.

- There are concerns that privatisation may lead to lower costs (improved **technical efficiency**) at the expense of the quality of output or even safety. Private cleaning firms, for example, can make more profit by lowering costs. This might be done by providing a lower standard of cleaning. **Administrative costs** are then incurred in drawing up contracts, which specify the standard of cleaning required, and then enforcing them. Many people thought that the privatisation of the rail network provided an incentive for firms to spend less money on track maintenance, making accidents more likely. This is why the government created Network Rail, a '**not for profit**' organisation to manage the rail infrastructure.

- The Private Finance Initiative (PFI) has been used to create excellent new facilities but without an immediate cost to the taxpayer, who instead pays for the facilities through a stream of rent payments over a long term lease. There are a number of issues here. One is about **equity** and whether this arrangement is fair to future generations of taxpayers. Another is about the long term value of the project and whether it will eventually be more expensive than if the government had borrowed money and paid to construct the facility itself. Finally, the cost versus quality issue discussed under the previous bullet point is also relevant here. Firms building PFI projects have an incentive to cut costs and, as a result, they will build a facility to the exact specification in the contract. This may not be to the same standard as a state managed project.

Deregulation

Deregulation involves the reduction of entry barriers to markets by the removal of legal restrictions. In recent years a number of statutory monopolies have been opened up to new competition. Examples include gas and electricity supply, bus services and directory enquiries.

Evaluating deregulation

- Deregulation is designed to improve **resource allocation**. This can occur in one of two ways. Deregulation makes the market more **contestable** and so the threat of new entry may force incumbent firms to reduce prices and increase output. Prices will also move closer to marginal cost. Alternatively, the lowering of entry barriers may result in new firms actually entering the market. The market then becomes less concentrated and monopoly power is reduced. As long as there are no other sources of **market failure** present (such as imperfect information, consumer inertia, or externalities) resource allocation should improve.

- To evaluate deregulation it is useful to look at real world examples such as the provision of directory enquiries. Since this service was opened up to new competition, a number of providers have spent very heavily on advertising. There is a risk that customers simply use the firm whose name (and number) they know best and that customers may have little **information** about which service is actually the cheapest.

- Deregulation is a vital complement to the privatisation of a state owned monopoly. Otherwise, a private monopoly has been created and the effects of this on market performance are likely to be damaging. If deregulation is not possible, then it is necessary for a regulatory body to oversee the pricing of the private monopoly.

- Deregulation of some utilities is difficult because they are **natural monopolies**. These are industries that can only efficiently support one firm because they have large infrastructures with very high fixed costs. Good examples include the supply of water, gas and electricity. Despite the fact that these industries are natural monopolies it has been possible to deregulate these markets. In the case of gas, National Grid owns the pipe network but has been forced by legislation to allow other providers to pay to use that network to supply gas. The price paid by these other providers to use the network is set by the industry regulator.

It should be noted, however, that while the gas and electricity markets initially became much more competitive following deregulation, subsequent merger and takeover activity has reduced the number of firms. **Consumer inertia** can also be a significant barrier to the efficient operation of gas and electricity markets. If consumers are reluctant to switch providers because it is seen as difficult or time consuming, this reduces any downward pressure on prices.

A typical average cost curve for a natural monopoly is shown in Figure 9.2.

Figure 9.2: Natural monopoly

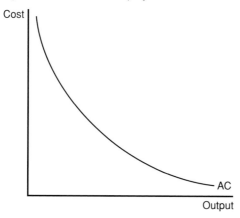

Internal markets

A belief in market principles may prompt governments to use internal markets in the delivery of public services such as education and health care.

In an internal market, different state schools or hospitals ('suppliers') must compete for custom: from parents choosing a school for their child or from GPs deciding where their patient is to be treated (the demand side). In education, schools receive funding per pupil they attract. In the NHS, GPs can be given budgets that they must decide how to spend on behalf of their patients.

The result is that resources follow consumer demand. Schools that fail to attract pupils will lack resources and failing schools may have to close. At the moment, state schools can compete only on quality, not on price, but this could change if parents were given a 'voucher' to spend on their child's education, which could be topped up with cash to buy a place at an expensive state school or a private school. Similarly, in an NHS internal market, GPs would choose hospitals for their patients based both on the price and quality of the service.

Evaluating internal markets

In favour	Against
• Poorly performing schools or hospitals are unlikely to survive. • Quality may be driven up as part of the competitive process. • Price competition may create greater efficiency as a result of a need to drive down costs (reduction in x-inefficiency).	• Poorly performing schools or hospitals may be deprived of the resources they need to improve. • Market failure may occur in the internal market, for example due to poor information for parents in choosing schools or GPs in selecting hospitals. • Some hospitals may have monopoly power if there is no other hospital nearby. • Schoolchildren and patients may have to travel considerable distances to the chosen institution.

Chapter

10

Unit 3: Introductory concepts → Markets generally work well → Sometimes markets fail
→ **This may justify government intervention** → Government failure sometimes occurs

Competition Policy

Competition policy

When concentrated markets fail to produce efficient outcomes, because of the monopoly power exercised by one or more firms, government intervention is likely. Competition policy involves government intervention to regulate markets to help them operate more efficiently.

The rationale for competition policy

The need for competition policy can be understood by studying the theoretical case against **monopoly**. More detail on this topic can be found in Chapter 5, but here we repeat the diagram comparing the efficiency (welfare) outcomes of monopoly and perfect competition. The monopoly equilibrium (Pm;Qm) sees the price forced above marginal cost, creating a **misallocation of resources** and a **deadweight welfare loss**. This is in comparison to the perfectly competitive equilibrium (Pc;Qc).

Figure 10.1: Deadweight welfare loss under monopoly

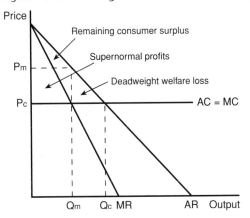

The public interest criterion

- Cases of **merger** or **takeover** are judged on the public interest criterion. The Competition Commission can investigate the effects of a merger or takeover that would create a firm with a combined market share of over 25%. If, on balance, they find that the merger will be detrimental to the public interest they can make a recommendation that the government blocks it. It is possible for **conditions** to be attached if a merger or takeover is allowed to proceed. For example, when Morrisons took over Safeway, the firm had to sell one store in towns where they would own two outlets.

- Cases of **implicit collusion** in oligopolistic markets can also be investigated by the Competition Commission to see if they damage the public interest, as can a variety of other **restrictive practices**. A restrictive practice is defined as a measure taken by a firm to limit competition in its market. One example is the retailer's recommended price (RRP) that has been used in the past by manufacturers of electrical goods in an effort to prevent retailers from driving down profit margins by competing on price. Where such measures are found to operate against the public interest, measures known as '**remedies**' are taken to help the market function more efficiently. In the case of extended warranties for electrical goods sold at the time an appliance is purchased, the remedies were as follows: stores had to advertise the right of the consumer to buy an extended warranty from other providers, the consumer would have the option to buy an extended warranty in the weeks following his/her purchase (not just at the till) and there would be a right of cancellation for the customer for 28 days afterwards.

Recent developments in Competition Policy

UK competition policy has been strengthened considerably in recent years. The 1998 Competition Act created a **prohibition** of:

● Abuse of a dominant position in a market.

● Anti-competitive agreements.

These changes bring UK competition policy into line with existing EU policy. The EU competition authorities deal with cases involving two or more companies located in different member states.

The offences covered by the act include serious **restrictive practices**, often involving price fixing, such as:

● **Cartel agreements** where colluding firms agree a set price enforced by a quota of output for each company.

● **Bid rigging** (where firms that regularly bid against each other for contracts take it in turns to win, but the winning bid is at an inflated price).

● **Refusal to supply** retailers who intend to sell products at a discount.

The 1998 Competition Act introduced fines of up to 10% of turnover for guilty companies. It also gave the Office of Fair Trading the authority to raid the offices of companies under suspicion (known as 'dawn raids') to look for evidence of anti-competitive behaviour. Still further, it was possible for 'whistleblowers' (firms who bring price-fixing to the attention of the authorities) to be exempted from penalties.

In 2002, the Enterprise Act introduced prison sentences for company directors found guilty of price fixing.

Deregulation

In some markets, all that is needed for a market to function efficiently is the removal of legal barriers that currently make markets difficult to enter. See Chapter 9 for further details.

Evaluating UK Competition Policy

Empirical evidence suggests that UK competition policy may have been effective in recent years. Price fixing cases are less frequent than they were and this may be due, at least in part, to the toughening of UK competition policy in 1998 and again in 2002. High profile cases such as those pursued against Argos, Littlewoods and Hasbro over the price fixing of board games and against Umbro over the pricing of Manchester United FC and England football shirts have set an example that may have deterred other firms. Competition in these markets is certainly more effective now than it was in the past. It is thought that the prohibitions introduced in 1998 have made UK competition policy much clearer.

The effectiveness of competition policy depends partly on the **information** available to the authorities and nowhere is this more the case than when the Competition Commission has to judge whether a monopoly, merger, or a restrictive practice, operates against the public interest. However, where the authorities are able to reach well informed judgements this should help improve the efficiency of **resource allocation**. It should be noted, that when judging the degree of competition in a market, the initial definition of a market is important. A narrow definition of a market (e.g. the cola market) may give the impression of a market less competitive than one that is more broadly defined (e.g. the carbonated drinks market or the soft drinks market).

Introducing regulation, as competition policy does, involves a significant **administrative cost**. However, given the role of competition policy in deterring high prices that are associated with low output, resource misallocation and deadweight welfare loss, it seems likely that competition policy improves economic efficiency and produces a net social benefit. As a result, the risk of **government failure** appears slight.

The electricity market is regulated by OFGEM.

Industry regulators

In a number of markets the government has introduced a permanent regulatory body to oversee the industry. These bodies are common in utility markets. There are industry regulators in the water industry (OFWAT), gas and electricity markets (OFGEM) and telephone, television and broadband services (OFCOM), for example. Their roles include:

● Price regulation.

● The promotion of competition (for example, by forcing mobile providers to allow customers to take their existing number to another firm; or by forcing firms to provide clear information about their prices for price comparison purposes).

● Enforcing standards of customer service.

● Ensuring customer safety.

● Encouraging investment (for example, less stringent price controls may be put in place for firms that reinvest a significant proportion of their profits).

● Promoting innovation.

Price regulation (with evaluation)

UK industry regulators have often used 'RPI + or − X' formulae to prevent utility firms from charging high prices. In essence this imposes a price ceiling (maximum price).

An 'RPI − X' formula implies that firms will have to make **real price cuts** by raising their prices more slowly than prices are increasing in the wider economy. Such restrictions were common in the years shortly after the utility providers were privatised.

An 'RPI + X' formula allows firms to make real price increases. This would typically be the case if the firm needed to raise revenue to pay for the maintenance of infrastructure, to invest in new capital or to undertake research and development. The water industry has often been allowed to raise its prices in order to pay for repairs to reduce leakages from the pipe network.

Regulating prices prevents firms from abusing a **dominant position** at the expense of the consumer. The restriction on price limits the revenue of firms, but has the advantage that they can still increase profit by becoming more **technically efficient** and reducing waste. This method is preferable to the regulation of profit, where the incentive to become more efficient is blunted. Regulators must be careful, however, not to punish firms for becoming more efficient and more profitable by tightening their formula too much. They must also ensure that the price they set is compatible with maintaining the safety and quality of service for customers.

The quality of regulation is highly dependent on the **information** available to regulators. Such information is provided by firms themselves or by making comparisons with other firms (e.g. comparing one regional water company to another. This is known as '**yardstick competition**'). Poor information leads to poor decision making, as in one case where Severn Trent Water under reported their profits. Based on this, the regulator allowed them to charge a higher price than should have been the case.

Concerns have been raised that there is a possibility of **regulatory capture**. This occurs where the regulator begins to serve the interests of firms in the market rather than the interests of consumers. It would be possible for regulatory capture to happen if a regulator built too close a relationship with firms, or if the regulator feared negative publicity (e.g. newspaper headlines such as "Electricity price cut threatens customer safety"). There is no clear evidence of regulatory capture in the UK, but it is a potential source of **government failure**.

Empirical evidence for the success of UK regulation comes from the fact that in many utilities regulators have ceased to set price controls. They judge that competition in the market is now sufficiently effective that it is not possible for firms to raise their price artificially.

Regulation by target setting

In recent years it has become common for regulators to set performance targets, both in the public and private sectors (e.g. for the length of time spent on a waiting list for NHS treatment or for the punctuality of trains).

Such target setting may provide an **incentive** to improve performance, especially if backed up by appropriate penalties for failing to meet the target. Drawbacks include the possibility that firms may reduce **quality** in order to hit the target (e.g. NHS operations may be hurried in order to fit more into a day). Those aspects of a firm's performance that are not subject to a target may deteriorate as resources are moved into the key target areas. There have been suggestions that the target of 5 A*-C grades for GCSE students has caused some schools to focus on pupils who are within reach of the target and not offer significant help to pupils who are really struggling.

Chapter 11

Unit 3: Introductory concepts → Markets generally work well → **Sometimes markets fail** → **This may justify government intervention** → **Government failure sometimes occurs**

Market Failure and Government Intervention

Market Failure for AS & A2 - Summary

Type of market failure	AS Level Analysis	A2 Extension	Appropriate Government Intervention
1. Monopoly power	Monopolists raise the price and restrict output compared to competitive markets, leading to a breakdown of the price mechanism and a misallocation of resources.	Study of the formal model of monopoly. Failure to achieve P = MC. Study of deadweight welfare loss from monopoly. Possibility of monopoly power in other concentrated markets (e.g. collusive oligopoly). An awareness of monopsony as sole buying power.	Regulation – A full knowledge of Competition Policy is required for A2. Deregulation as a means of making markets more contestable.
2. Externalities	Third party effects not accounted for by the price mechanism. Missing markets.	No significant extensions. A study of environmental externalities is useful for AQA and those related to transport if you are studying OCR's transport option.	Indirect taxation (negative externalities). Subsidies (positive externalities). Extending property rights. Pollution permits.
3. Merit/Demerit goods	Goods which are under- and over-provided by the market mechanism respectively, for reasons such as failure to account for externalities and the discounting of future costs/benefits.	Understanding of the MSB = MSC condition for optimal resource allocation (this was already covered at AS level by AQA students).	Indirect taxation (demerit goods). Subsidies (merit goods). State provision (merit goods). Regulation (demerit goods).
4. Public goods	Goods which are both non-rivalrous and non-excludable leading to the free rider problem. Missing markets.	Knowledge of quasi public goods (typically non-rivalrous, but excludable – such as television signals). Public good aspects of the environment (e.g. air) useful for AQA.	State provision. Extending property rights in the case of public goods aspects of the environment. Pollution permits.
5. Imperfect knowledge	Prevents consumers from making utility maximising decisions.	Further applications of imperfect knowledge (e.g. in utility markets looking at privatisation, deregulation and competition policy). An awareness of consumer inertia as an additional source of market failure.	Measures to improve consumer knowledge and make switching between providers easier. Industry regulators play a key part in this in utility markets.
6. Resource immobility	Immobile resources preventing firms from responding to price signals.	No significant extensions. Application to macro in understanding immobility as a source of structural unemployment.	Education and training in the case of occupational labour immobility. Measures to improve flows of information (e.g. about job vacancies).
7. Unstable commodity prices	Volatile prices as a source of unpredictable living standards for producers; resulting in difficulty in business planning; difficulties for consumers arising from volatility.	No extensions.	Buffer stock schemes.
8. A lack of equity	Unfair outcomes as a source of market failure, e.g. an unfair distribution of income. Contrasts with other sources of a market failure in that it is normative in nature while the others are positive.	Detailed study of the determinants of income distribution and causes of poverty for AQA and for OCR option on Work & Leisure. Understanding of the terms vertical and horizontal equity.	Maximum prices (equity for consumers). Minimum prices (equity for suppliers). Universal and means-tested benefits. Progressive taxation.

A2 units are synoptic in nature. They build and extend on the theory covered at AS level. It is important that students retain an understanding of market failure and government intervention and appreciate how the material studied in Unit 3 builds upon this. The summary table on the previous page is designed to help in this regard.

One important area of study for market failure at A2 is the environment, especially when you are following the AQA specification.

Environmental market failure

Environmental market failures relate to the factor of production – land. Land is defined as all the resources found in the natural environment.

Types of environmental market failure: (1) Resource Depletion

Resource depletion occurs when there are fewer natural resources available compared to previous time periods. This is inevitably the case for **non-renewable resources** such as fossil fuels, which are not replaced as they are used. It may also be the case for some **renewable resources**, such as fish or trees, if they are used at a faster rate than they can be renewed. Resource depletion can be seen as a **negative externality** with future generations being the third parties (an MSB/MSC diagram would be appropriate).

(2) Resource degradation

Resource degradation occurs when a natural resource is rendered less productive than it was in previous time periods. For example, this could be the result of air or water pollution, or over farming. Resource degradation can be seen as a **negative externality** with future generations being seen as the third parties.

(3) Public good aspects of the environment

Some aspects of the environment, notably the air, can be considered public goods. This is because air is **non-rivalrous**, **non-excludable** (and **non-rejectable** too) and, as a result, the free rider problem applies. No economic agent is likely to bear the cost of cleaning up the air (or refraining from polluting it) because the benefits cannot be confined to those bearing the cost. Government intervention is likely to be necessary if clean air is desired.

(4) Negative externalities

Many environmental market failures are associated with **third party costs** not reflected in market prices. A classic example of this is pollution (air, water, visual and noise). Goods associated with pollution in production or consumption are likely to be **over provided** by the market.

(5) Positive externalities

In contrast, the market is unlikely to produce in sufficient quantities those goods and services carrying positive environmental externalities, such as the planting of trees or the availability of open green spaces.

It is important to apply AS level knowledge of government intervention to questions about the environment, e.g. in evaluating the use of indirect taxation or regulation in tackling environmental issues.

Additionally, it is very helpful to have a deeper understanding of tradable pollution permits than was required for AS level and to appreciate the importance of property rights.

Property rights

Negative externalities arise largely from the fact that nobody owns the environment and it is therefore free to use.

Consider the example of a chemical factory that discharges its waste products into a local river. This kills some fish, negatively affecting third parties in the form of the local fishing club who use the river.

Allocating ownership of the river to the fishing club would produce an efficient outcome. Where the benefit to the chemical company of polluting the river exceeded the cost to the fishing club of allowing that pollution, the chemical company would be able to compensate the fishing club and both parties would be better off. This would work the other way round if ownership of the river were given to the chemical firm. In either case, all mutually beneficial trades would be undertaken and the **socially optimal** level of pollution found.

Evaluating the extension of property rights

The extension of property rights is a theoretically simple method of achieving an efficient economic outcome, as the externality is successfully **internalised** (brought back within the market system). If the fishing club owns the river, the chemical company is forced to pay for the pollution it generates.

There is no need for the regulatory authorities to try to make any artificial judgements about the optimal level of pollution. Indeed it is for this reason that extending property rights is often thought to be an effective and superior alternative to regulating pollution. However, it will be necessary legally to protect the property rights of the owners of environmental resources. This itself carries an administrative cost and may be difficult.

There are **equity** considerations. The optimal level of pollution will be found regardless of who is allocated ownership of the river, but this decision affects the **distribution of income and wealth**: you are better off if you own something than if you don't. An option is for the government to auction the property rights in the first instance, thereby generating revenue.

Tradable pollution permits

An alternative to the full allocation of property rights is for governments to cap pollution at what they judge to be the optimal level. Firms are then allocated permits to allow them to emit a certain level of pollution in an agreed time period (say a year), but can sell any permits that they do not need to other firms. Such '**emissions trading**' or '**cap and trade**' schemes have become increasingly prominent and have extended to international agreements, where countries have permits to produce agreed levels of pollution but can sell these permits to other countries if they wish.

Evaluating tradable pollution permits

The key advantages of pollution permits are that:

● Those firms or countries that find it least costly to control pollution will do so and then sell their spare permits to those who find it most expensive. Therefore this is the most **efficient** way of reaching the desired level of pollution.

● International cap and trade schemes can be used to address injustices in the **international distribution of income**. If poor countries are allocated sufficient permits, they can sell them to richer countries that wish to carry on polluting. The effect is that the richer countries compensate the poorer nations for the pollution generated.

● As with the allocation of property rights, what was previously an externality (outside the market) has been **internalised** and those who pollute now have to pay for their activities (the '**polluter pays principle**').

Pollution permits internalise externalities so that polluters are made to pay.

The disadvantages of pollution permits are that:

● The scheme does require a judgement to be reached about the optimal level of pollution. There is probably not sufficient **information** to reach this judgement accurately.

● A new market in pollution permits has been created and this market itself may be subject to **market failures**.

● The trading of permits affects the geographical distribution of pollution. Some pollutants may cause more damage if they are heavily concentrated in one geographical area, rather than being more widely spread.

It is possible for the authorities to reduce the number of permits in circulation over time in order to meet environmental targets. This effectively increases the price of polluting as shown by the price rise from P1 to P2 in Figure 11.1.

Figure 11.1: The effects of reducing the supply of pollution permits

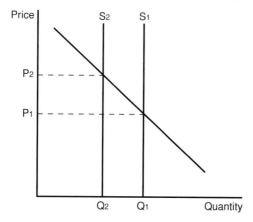

Government failure

It is vital to retain an understanding of government failure from AS level and be able to apply it in A2 contexts. Government failure occurs when the cost of an intervention exceeds the benefits of intervention and, as a result, worsens resource allocation. The most likely causes of government failure are:

● **High administrative costs resulting from government intervention.** Competition policy carries a significant administration cost (though possibly not one which exceeds its benefits). For example, the high costs of maintaining the Competition Commission, Office for Fair Trading and industry regulators.

● **Inadequate information.** Regulators may make the wrong decisions if they have insufficient or inadequate information. For example, industry regulators need accurate information to judge whether a firm's profit levels are excessive and are an exploitation of their monopoly power.

● **Unintended consequences.** For example, regulation to prevent overfishing has caused fishermen to throw fish back into the sea, even though the fish are already dead, because the fishermen have exceeded their quota.

● **Conflict between objectives.** The potential for an **equity-efficiency trade off** is an example of such a conflict. Consider the role of the regulator in trying to ensure competitive prices in gas and electricity markets. This might conflict with environmental objectives that would require higher prices. Conflict between economic and political objectives may also occur.

Chapter 12

Unit 3: Introductory concepts → Markets generally work well → Sometimes markets fail → **This may justify government intervention** → Government failure sometimes occurs

Cost-Benefit Analysis

Cost-Benefit Analysis

Cost-Benefit Analysis (CBA) is a method used to appraise major investment projects. A project is **commercially viable** if its private benefits exceed its private costs, but a CBA attempts to establish whether the project carries a **net social benefit** (net social benefit = social benefit − social cost). Governments may choose to carry out a CBA to help improve **resource allocation**. Examples of projects suitable for a CBA include the building of a new line on the London Underground, a new runway at a major airport or a nuclear power station. The decision to bid for the Olympic Games in London would also have been a suitable candidate for a CBA.

Figure 12.1 is useful for illustrating the reason for carrying out a CBA. The wish is to ensure that the project is an efficient (socially optimal) use of resources. The social optimum is illustrated as Q* in the diagrams. This occurs where the MSB = MSC.

In the case of positive externalities, the private optimum would be at output Q, where MPB = MPC and there would be an under consumption of the good or service. In the case of negative externalities, the private optimum would also be at Q, but this time there would be an over production of the good or service.

Figure 12.1: Social optimality

Positive externalities

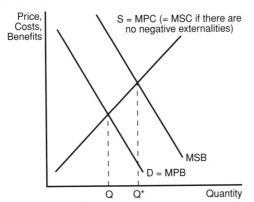

Negative externalities

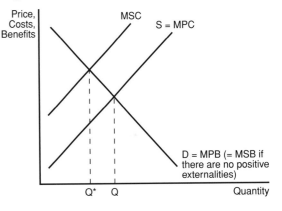

The method of CBA

The method for carrying out a CBA is as follows:

1. Identify all the costs and benefits involved with the project. This includes both the private costs and benefits and the external costs and benefits (third party effects not accounted for in market prices).

2. Attach a monetary value to each cost and benefit.

3. Find the social benefit and social cost of the project using:

   Social benefit = private benefit + external benefit

   Social cost = private cost + external cost

4. Subtract the social cost from the social benefit in order to find the net social benefit of the project.

5. Use the principle of **opportunity cost**. Look at alternative uses for the resources, or at other projects that could be undertaken in order to establish whether the project is the best use of the resources.

Problems with CBA (1): Identifying all costs and benefits

Governments may not possess the **information** to identify accurately each cost and benefit associated with a project. There may be unforeseen consequences of pressing ahead with the project that, by their nature, cannot be included in the CBA.

Problems with CBA (2): Putting a monetary value on costs and benefits

Private benefits and costs are valued by market transactions and therefore may seem relatively easy to measure. The private benefits of a new line on the London Underground, for example, would include faster journey times and easier access to destinations. These benefits are measured by the amount that the users are willing to pay and therefore by the revenue generated for the operator. Similarly, the private costs of the project can be measured in terms of the money paid out for construction and then later for maintenance and operating costs, such as staffing.

However, future demand may turn out to be higher or lower than expected, while costs may also be hard to estimate. Major investment projects have a habit of exceeding their planned budget during construction, and maintenance and operating costs may also be tricky to forecast.

Externalities are more difficult to put a value on because they are not priced by market transactions. The table below suggests some methods for valuing common externalities and some of the problems entailed.

Externality	Possible methods for valuing	Difficulties entailed
Congestion	Multiply hours of congestion by national average wage.	Is road use actually skewed towards those who earn more than the average wage? Does it matter whether the lost hours are work or leisure time?
Air pollution	Value at cost of treating respiratory illnesses caused by the pollution and the value of any lost hours of work.	Fails to account for the impact of respiratory illness on the quality of life of those who suffer.
Noise pollution	Measure the lost value of houses located close to source of noise (e.g. busy road); use survey data – how much would sufferers need to be compensated to accept the source of the noise if they had a choice about it?	Survey data is unreliable – people may not give accurate information when faced by a hypothetical choice.
Loss of human life	Multiply remaining years of working life by the national average annual wage.	Valuing human life raises ethical issues; The method suggested seems to discount the value of leisure time and the years spent in retirement.
Multiplier effects	Estimate the benefit to the economy as a result of 'second round spending' (e.g. spending by workers employed in the project).	The value of the multiplier depends heavily on how much of the spending leaks from the circular flow: how much will be saved, taxed or spent on imports?

Problems with CBA (3): Valuing costs or benefits that may or may not occur

Some of the costs and benefits to be included in a CBA will be things that might or might not occur. For example, when conducting a CBA on the building of a nuclear power station, for example, the possibility of a catastrophic nuclear accident should be considered.

To deal with this situation, it is necessary to attach a **probability** to the cost or benefit concerned. For example, there may be a 0.001 chance of a nuclear accident. The cost of the accident should it occur would then have to be multiplied by this probability to calculate what is called an **expected value**.

Problems with CBA (4): Valuing costs or benefits that occur in the future

Investment projects produce streams of costs and benefits over a long period of time. Given the choice between £100 now or £100 in ten years time, we would all choose £100 now: money has more value in the present than in the future.

It is necessary, therefore, to **discount** future costs and benefits to find their present value. The difficulty is in choosing an **appropriate rate of discount**: should the value of costs and benefits be reduced by 3, 4 or 5% for each year they occur into the future or by some other figure? The value chosen may make a significant difference to the outcome of the CBA.

Many CBA studies place a time limit on the costs and benefits to be included (e.g. those that occur over the next 20 years) because costs or benefits occurring further into the future than this may be too difficult to predict or value.

Evaluating a CBA

Given the uncertainties outlined in the previous sections, the results of a CBA should be treated with caution. Whether a CBA should be carried out depends on how useful the information it provides is, relative to the cost of undertaking the CBA.

To increase the value of the information provided by the CBA it is necessary to:

- Ensure that the CBA is carried out independently and its assumptions are not biased by political considerations.

- State clearly where it has not been possible to place a monetary value on any costs or benefits.

- State clearly the assumptions that have been made in valuing costs and benefits, such as the discount rate used.

- Conduct a **sensitivity analysis**, looking at the effect on the outcome of the CBA if its assumptions are varied. It may be possible to ask different teams of economists to conduct separate CBAs. They will doubtless use different assumptions but, if all agree that the project carries a significant net social benefit or cost, this gives more confidence in the conclusion.

It should be noted that conducting a CBA is itself a significant **administrative cost** that may run into many millions of pounds and is therefore a potential source of **government failure** if the CBA does not produce useful information.

It is unlikely that a CBA would be used as the sole determinant as to whether to go ahead with the project, but rather that it is used as a source of information to inform the decision. It is possible to argue that undertaking a major investment without a full consideration of its likely impact would be irresponsible on the part of a government and at least a CBA ensures a careful study of the costs and benefits.

Real world examples can be informative. A CBA was carried out to help decide whether to build a third runway at Heathrow Airport. It produced a conclusion that the net social benefit would be £47 million per year. This is a small **rate of return** when expressed as a percentage of the multi billion pound costs of the project. It would not need major changes to the assumptions of the CBA to turn this into a net social cost.

In the 1970s, when the British and French governments decided to plough billions into the Concorde project they chose not to do a CBA. The aircraft revenue streams turned out to be smaller than expected, the costs were greater than anticipated and, in 2003, Concorde took its last flight. It is likely that the project carried a large net social cost and it is possible that a CBA may have produced useful information that would have prevented the project from ever starting.

Chapter 13

Unit 3: Introductory concepts → **Markets generally work well** → Sometimes markets fail → This may justify government intervention → Government failure sometimes occurs

Wage Determination

There is no material on labour markets in Edexcel's Unit 3 specification. This chapter is therefore aimed at those studying for the AQA exam or OCR's option on 'Work and Leisure'.

Wages

Wages are the reward to labour as a factor of production. They compensate workers for giving up their leisure time. Thus the **opportunity cost** of an hour of leisure time is the wage foregone.

Labour supply

The choice between work and leisure is crucial to labour supply.

It is sometimes argued that individuals have **backward bending labour supply curves** as shown in Figure 13.1(a). This is the result of adding together two distinct effects on labour supply to find the effect of a wage increase:

Substitution effect

As wages rise, the opportunity cost of leisure time increases. This provides a greater incentive to work and encourages more labour supply as workers substitute away from leisure.

Income effect

Wage increases have the effect of increasing total pay earned from any given number of hours worked. Workers who are already enjoying high wages may have a **target income** that they have already reached. They then respond to wage increases by taking more leisure time while maintaining their target income.

However, the labour supply to any particular occupation is likely to be a conventional upward sloping supply curve, as in Figure 13.1(b). Even if individuals already working in a market may respond to wage increases by working fewer hours, higher wages will attract new entrants to the occupation (including some workers moving across from other jobs).

Figure 13.1(a): Individual labour supply

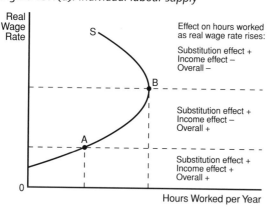

Figure 13.1(b): Occupational labour supply

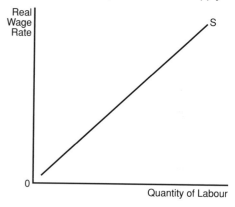

Labour is a derived demand

It is important to remember that firms demand labour not for its own sake but because of the output that it produces. Thus labour demand is a derived demand: when demand for the product made by a firm rises, so too does its demand for labour.

Marginal Revenue Product (MRP)

Marginal revenue product (**MRP**) is the revenue generated for the firm by employing one extra worker. It is the result of the worker's marginal (physical) product (**MPP**) and the marginal revenue (**MR**) derived from each additional unit sold:

$$MRP = MPP \times MR$$

Look back to Chapter 1 for a reminder on how the marginal (physical) product curve is shaped first of all by gains from specialisation and then by diminishing returns. If the firm sells its product in a perfectly competitive market, then marginal revenue is constant at the prevailing market price (P), so:

$$MRP = MPP \times P$$

This means that the MRP curve has the same basic shape as the MPP curve, because it is simply the MPP multiplied by a constant factor.

Firms would be willing to take on an extra worker as long as the worker's MRP exceeded the cost to the firm of taking him/her on. If the labour market is perfectly competitive, the cost to the firm of taking on an extra worker is simply the wage (W), so:

Extra workers are employed up to the point where: **MRP = W**.

The MRP curve plots the number of workers (quantity of labour) against the MRP of the last worker. It is also the labour demand curve, given the condition above.

Wage determination

Figure 13.2 shows a model of wage determination in a competitive market. The wage (W) is set by supply and demand in the occupational labour market, such as the market for accountants. The individual accountancy firm is then a wage taker and must accept the wage set in the occupational labour market, choosing to employ all workers with an MRP that is greater than the wage. It will, therefore, employ workers up to quantity q in Figure 13.2(b).

Figure 13.2: Wage determination

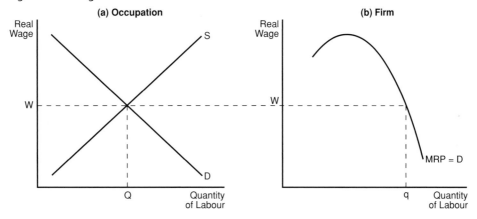

Elasticity of labour supply and demand	**Sensitivity of labour demand to wage increases (elasticity of demand) is high if:**	**Sensitivity of labour supply to wage increases (elasticity of supply) is high if:**
	• Capital is easily used instead of labour. • Wages form a high proportion of total costs. • The price of the product is sensitive to wage costs and the demand for the product is elastic.	• Work is relatively unskilled. • Training periods are short. • There are other occupations that use similar skills. • There are few non-monetary rewards to the work.

Wage differentials

If the labour market for the economy as a whole were perfectly competitive, everyone would be paid the same. In such a market, all workers would possess the same skills, so if the wages of airline pilots were higher than those of lorry drivers, the supply of pilots would rise as lorry drivers switched occupations. The wages of pilots would fall and those of lorry drivers would rise (due to reduced supply) until the gap in pay was eliminated.

However, wage rates **do** differ, and the reason for this must be labour market imperfections, such as:

● **Each worker is unique** (labour is not homogenous). This causes wage differentials in three ways:

　1. Workers have different marginal revenue products and, as a result, the demand for different types of labour varies;

2. Workers have different skills and preferences and, as a result, the supply of different types of labour varies;

3. Workers may experience discrimination.

● **Market forces tend to equalise net benefits to workers rather than wages.** Non-monetary benefits from a job (such as vocational satisfaction) tend to increase labour supply and reduce wages. Factors such as danger or unpleasant working conditions serve to reduce labour supply and increase the wage. These effects on wages are sometimes known as '**compensating differentials**'.

● **Labour is not perfectly mobile**: either geographically or occupationally.

● Lack of competition on the supply side due to trade unions (see Chapter 14). A strong trade union can raise wages for its workers.

● Lack of competition on the demand side if there is a **powerful monopsonist employer**. An employer who accounts for all, or a substantial share, of the employment in a labour market can use their power to drive down wages.

Example: Why do premiership footballers get paid more than nurses?

Reasons for this include:

● The MRP of footballers is very high (gate receipts, television revenue, merchandising).

● EU legislation means players can move at the end of their contracts without a transfer fee being paid. The money that a club would have been willing to pay in a transfer fee is now likely to be paid to the player in wages (up to the point where W = MRP).

● Some clubs are willing to pay a wage higher than MRP for top players. This is likely at clubs with rich owners, willing to run the club at a loss in order to pursue footballing success.

● The fact that labour is not homogeneous is especially apparent in relation to footballers. The special skills that some players possess enable them to earn enormous amounts of money.

● The supply of footballers with the talent to play in the Premiership is low and inelastic. When labour supply is inelastic, high levels of demand create higher wages rather than greater employment, as shown in Figure 13.3.

Figure 13.3: Wages of Premiership footballers

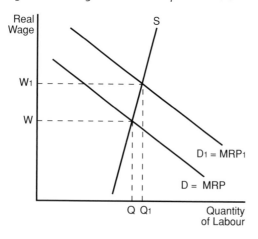

● The monopsonist power of the state in relation to the hiring of nurses helps depress wages.

● The vocational element of nursing leads to nurses being paid less than they otherwise would (a negative compensating differential).

● Nurses' unions are reluctant to strike. This lessens their bargaining power.

Chapter

14

Unit 3: Introductory concepts → Markets generally work well → **Sometimes markets fail** → This may justify government intervention → Government failure sometimes occurs

Trade Unions and Monopsony Employers

Trade unions and monopsony employers

There is no material on labour markets in Edexcel's Unit 3 specification. This chapter is therefore aimed at those studying for the AQA exam or OCR's option on 'Work and Leisure'.

One of the key roles of trade unions is to seek better pay for their members. They do this by **collective bargaining** with management, with the pay for a group of workers decided by a single negotiation. This is a **market imperfection** as the supply side of the labour market is no longer competitive. Unions also attempt to improve other aspects of the working lives of their members, including fringe benefits, working conditions and job security.

Monopsony employers are a sign of lack of competition on the demand side of the labour market. This describes a situation where a single firm accounts for all, or a substantial proportion, of the employment in a labour market. In the UK, the state can be considered a monopsonist employer of teachers and health care professionals.

Effect of a trade union on wages and employment

For analysis, it is common to assume a '**closed shop**' where every worker in an occupation has to be a member of a single union. The result is that the firm will not receive a supply of labour unless it accepts the wage demands of that union.

Union density is said to be 100% in the case of a closed shop. Where the proportion of the workforce that are union members is less than 100%, or where membership is fragmented between a number of unions, this tends to reduce union power – the union acts as a monopoly supplier of labour.

The impact of a closed shop trade union is shown in Figure 14.1. The effective labour supply curve (Se) is perfectly elastic at the wage demanded by the union (Wtu) but beyond the kink in the curve higher wages are necessary to elicit further extensions of supply. There are two clear results. Firstly, the wage is higher than it would have been at Wc in a competitive labour market. Secondly, the higher wage causes a contraction of labour demand and an extension of labour supply. This causes excess supply of labour (unemployment). The extent of this unemployment depends on the elasticity of labour demand.

Figure 14.1: Trade unions

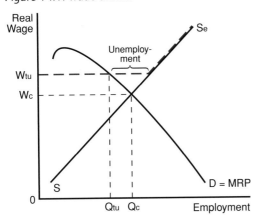

A measure of the success of unions in achieving higher wages for their members is the **union mark up**. This is the percentage by which the wages of union members exceed those of non-union members who are doing the same or comparable work.

Trade unions can actually protect jobs when countering the power of a monopsonist employer.

Effect of a monopsony on wages and employment

A monopsonist is **not** a **wage taker**. As the occupation's sole employer it is faced with the occupational supply curve. With its powerful position, it can choose any point on that curve. However, the implication of the curve is that if the monopsonist wishes to attract an extra worker it will have to pay a higher wage rate to all workers. The marginal cost of employing an extra worker (MCL) in Figure 14.2 is then greater than the average cost (ACL), namely the wage.

The monopsonist employer is expected to hire an extra worker as long as MRP > MCL so that the additional worker adds to profits. This is shown in Figure 14.2, with the result that the monopsonist hires Qm units of labour, but pays the lowest possible wage for this quantity, Wm. Note that this wage is below the MRP of the last worker. The extent to which this is true in any occupation can be used as a measure of monopsony power. It is clear that a monopsonist reduces both wage levels and employment in comparison to a competitive labour market (Wc, Qc)

Figure 14.2: Monopsony employers

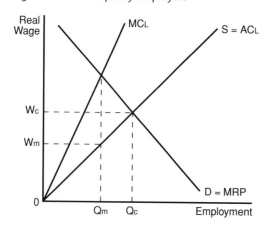

Trade unions and monopsony in the same market (bilateral monopoly)

The mechanics of a monopsonistic labour market are different when a trade union is present. A closed shop trade union renders the monopsonist once again a wage taker (see Wm+tu in Figure 14.3). Qm+tu union members are willing to supply their labour at this wage. Beyond this, a higher wage paid to all workers would be necessary to elicit further extensions of labour supply. This raises the marginal cost of hiring labour; producing a vertical discontinuity in the effective MCL curve as shown.

At the wage Wm+tu the monopsonist chooses to employ Qm+tu workers. This is more than the firm would have employed without the union present (Qm) and therefore the accusation that unions destroy jobs is not necessarily valid. The reason for this increase in employment is that the monopsonist, having been rendered a wage-taker, can employ additional workers at Wm+tu without having to pay a higher wage to all workers.

Figure 14.3: Bilateral monopoly

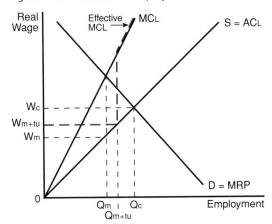

Do trade unions necessarily destroy jobs? (evaluation)

The actions of trade unions may not always destroy jobs. The following points may be used to support such a view:

● Higher wages may have a minimal effect on employment if labour demand is **inelastic** (for example, because it is difficult to substitute capital for labour or if labour costs are a small proportion of the total).

● Trade unions can actually protect jobs when they are countering the power of a monopsonist employer. There is some degree of monopsony power present in most labour markets. This can be measured by the extent to which wages are below MRP.

● Trade unions may help raise morale amongst workers by improving pay and conditions. It is possible that this may improve labour productivity, making workers more valuable to employers, and therefore less likely to be laid off as a result of the higher union wage.

● Unionised workers may not have the same need to switch jobs in search of better conditions as other workers. This reduces employment costs such as recruitment and training costs for firms which in turn may help protect jobs.

Chapter

15

Unit 3: Introductory concepts → Markets generally work well → **Sometimes markets fail** → **This may justify government intervention** → **Government failure sometimes occurs**

Income, Wealth and Poverty

There is no material on labour markets in Edexcel's Unit 3 specification. This chapter is therefore aimed at those studying for the AQA exam or OCR's option on 'Work and Leisure'.

Wealth

Wealth consists of a stock of assets (houses, cars, pension rights and savings, for example) with a marketable value. It is measured at a specific point in time. Strictly speaking, human capital could be considered part of wealth as well, but it does not have a marketable value as such.

Income

Income is a flow concept measured over a period of time. The flow of income is derived from the stock of assets that form wealth, e.g. human capital is used in earning wages, and interest is earned on savings.

The distribution of income

Data on the distribution of income is usually presented in deciles (where the top decile is the top ten per cent of income earners) or quintiles (where the top quintile is the top 20%). The same can be done with data for wealth.

The Lorenz Curve

The Lorenz Curve is a graphical representation of inequality.

The curve plots the percentage of a nation's income that is enjoyed by the poorest 'x' percent of the population. The axes are labelled 'cumulative'. For example, the poorest 15% of the population clearly include the poorest 10%.

The diagonal on the Lorenz Curve (see Figure 15.1) represents complete equality (50% of the population with 50% of the income and so on). Total inequality would see a curve running along the horizontal axis, from left to right, and then up the vertical. The further the Lorenz Curve bows away from the diagonal, the greater the degree of inequality. In Figure 15.1, the degree of inequality is greater in part (b) of the diagram.

Figure 15.1(a): Lorenz Curve

Figure 15.1(b): Lorenz Curve showing more inequality

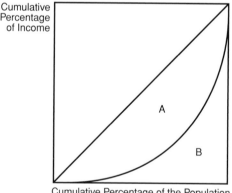

The Gini Coefficient

The Gini Coefficient is a numerical representation of inequality, derived from the Lorenz Curve. Using Figure 15.1:

Gini Coefficient = Area A/(Area A + Area B)

Gini values range from zero (complete equality) to one, or 100% (total inequality).

Lorenz Curves and Gini Coefficients can be applied to the distribution of wealth as well as to the distribution of income.

Factors affecting the distribution of income	Factors affecting the distribution of income include: ● **Wage differentials.** Those with high level qualifications and skills tend to generate high marginal revenue product (MRP) for their employers. It is also the case that such people are in limited and inelastic supply. Further, the increasing skill demands of the modern economy are putting a premium on the wages of skilled workers. This can be illustrated by an appropriate diagram (see Figure 13. 3). ● **Differences in income earned from assets.** The most important are financial assets such as savings and stock market investments, which yield interest and dividends to those who own them. ● **Age.** The distribution of income is skewed by age. The earnings potential of workers tends to peak in their 40s and 50s when they are rewarded for their work experience. ● **The influence of government policy.** Governments tend to operate a **progressive** system of taxation (which takes a higher proportion of income from those who earn more) and redistribute income through the benefit system. **Means-tested benefits** (available only to those on low incomes and those with few assets) have the greatest effect on distribution of income but **universal benefits** (available to all) also have an impact.
Why is wealth more unequally distributed than income?	Wealth tends to be more unequally distributed than income. Key reasons for this include: ● The **cumulative nature of wealth**. Those with valuable assets can derive high levels of income. The excess of income over expenditure then adds to wealth. Accumulated wealth is passed down through the generations by inheritance. ● **Pension rights** are the second biggest type of wealth in the UK after housing. Those individuals whose jobs carry generous pension entitlements (such as public sector workers, whose incomes might actually be lower than they would be in the private sector) therefore gain in wealth relative to others. ● Over time, **asset prices have tended to rise faster than incomes**. Consider housing, for example, where an inelastic supply sees prices rise significantly when the income elastic demand for housing increases. ● **Wealth is less easy to redistribute than income.** Although wealth can be taxed, it is often used for things such as benefit payments (which affect the distribution of income). It is not usual to give assets directly to the poorer members of society, although in theory this could be done. The sale of council houses at below market values to their tenants is an example.
Absolute poverty	Absolute poverty affects those who are so poor that their **basic needs** (food, water, clothing, shelter and sanitation) are not met and whose continued survival is threatened. The World Bank uses income thresholds of $1 or $2 a day to measure absolute poverty.
Relative poverty	Relative poverty affects those who are poor relative to others in their society. It is typically measured relative to median income, using a threshold such as 40 or 50% of the median. Those in relative poverty may or may not also be in absolute poverty.
The causes of poverty	The causes of poverty include: ● **Low wages**, affecting those with few skills and qualifications and hence a low MRP. Supply of such labour tends to be plentiful. ● **Unemployment.** Those affected are likely to be well below the median income level in society, although benefit payments may stave off absolute poverty.

- **Changing patterns of demand for labour.** This is related to the two points above. For example, the decline of UK manufacturing has left those with specific non-transferable skills **structurally unemployed** (long term). Meanwhile, increased demand for skilled workers has boosted their wages and, therefore, increased relative poverty.

- **Single parenthood**, which is increasing as a percentage of all parents in the UK. The household has only one potential wage earner, who may be unable to work in the absence of affordable childcare. Single parents who do work may spend a significant proportion of the wages they have earned on childcare.

- **Longer life spans.** As life expectancy increases (due to an improved diet and better healthcare), it is necessary to finance more years of retirement from the pension funds built up. This reduces the annual income yielded from the fund and reduces the income of pensioners.

The poverty trap and effective marginal tax rates

The poverty trap refers to a **disincentive to work**. It affects those in poverty and is created by the interaction of:

- Means tested benefits, which may be withdrawn as higher income is earned **and**

- Progressive taxation, which takes a higher percentage of income as more income is earned.

In the extreme, those on low incomes may face **effective marginal tax rates** of greater than 100% (where earning an additional £1 of income results in a combined payment of taxes and a loss of benefits that is greater than £1).

If unemployment benefit is sufficiently high, the **replacement ratio** (ratio of income when out of work to income when in work) may be close to or greater than one. The incentive to work is either reduced or removed completely.

The poverty trap is a possible example of **government failure** occurring from a **conflict of objectives** between equity (alleviating poverty) and efficiency (appropriate incentives to work).

Evaluating measures to tackle poverty

Ways to tackle the poverty trap include:

- Withdrawing benefits altogether. This is generally regarded as undesirable because of the adverse impact it will have on the distribution of income.

- Switching to universal rather than means tested benefits. Universal benefits are given to broad categories of people with no tests of their means or needs. Good examples include family allowances and the basic state pension. When a payment, such as family allowance, is provided regardless of income, the benefit will not target those most in need. Universal benefits are also very expensive.

- Withdrawing means-tested benefits only gradually as additional income is earned. This policy is more affordable and should provide a good incentive to work to those who are on low incomes.

Government interventions to tackle poverty often focus on the **redistribution of income** and are usually evaluated in terms of factors such as:

- The effect on incentives to work. For example, will a policy discourage workers from taking a job or working additional hours?

- Targeting – will the policy provide support to those groups who need it the most?

- Expense – this relates to the cost of the policy to the government.

- Take up rates – these refer to the proportion of those who are entitled to receive support who actually claim a benefit.

- Stigma – does receiving the benefit affect the reputation of the recipient?

In summary:

	Incentives to work	Targeting	Expense	Take-up rates	Stigma
Means-tested benefits	✗	✓	✓	✗	✗
Universal benefits	✓	✗	✗	✓	✓
Progressive taxation	✗	Not applicable			

✓ Favourable or neutral impact   ✗ Detrimental impact

In the long term, tackling poverty may require equipping a broader cross section of society with modern, relevant skills. Such supply side policies would also have macroeconomic benefits (increasing capacity and economic growth) but these benefits are not easy to achieve.

The national minimum wage

The national minimum wage (NMW) has played a significant role in the fight against poverty in recent years. Arguments in favour and against include:

In favour of the NMW	Against the NMW
The NMW will help alleviate poverty for those who receive it.	Raising wages leads to a contraction of labour demand and creates unemployment (the extent depends on elasticity of labour demand).
NMW offers a greater incentive to work for those who receive it.	Any unemployment created will disproportionately affect the young, whose inexperience results in a lower MRP.
A morale boost from higher wages could lead to a productivity boost.	The NMW raises the costs of firms and may make them uncompetitive in international markets.
The NMW should help reduce labour turnover at companies, lowering recruitment and training costs.	The NMW is potentially inflationary, especially if higher earners seek wage increases to restore differentials.
Firms paying more to their workers have a stronger incentive to train them, raising MRP.	The NMW fails to take account of regional differences in the cost of living.
The NMW can help to counter the power of monopsonist employers.	The NMW is not well targeted. Many recipients are second wage earners in their household and therefore not in poverty. Many who need help are unemployed and therefore do not benefit from the NMW.
Recipients of the NMW are disproportionately female. Male/female wage differentials are reduced.	Many recipients of the minimum wage are employed by the state, thus affecting public sector finances.

INCREASING MARKET CONCENTRATION →

	Perfect Competition	Monopolistic Competition	Oligopoly	Monopoly
Characteristics	• Many buyers, many sellers • Homogeneous products • No entry or exit barriers • Perfect knowledge of market conditions for all market participants	• As perfect competition, except: • Products are slightly differentiated	• A high concentration ratio • Interdependence • Barriers to entry are usually present	• One firm only • Barriers to entry high enough to prevent new entry
Long-Run Equilibrium			There is no uniquely defined long run equilibrium as such under oligopoly, because of the unpredictability generated by the interaction of the strategies of the firms in the market.	
Conduct and Performance	• All firms are price takers • Normal profit for all firms in long run (but short run losses or supernormal profit are possible) • Production at minimum AC (productive efficiency) and P = MC (allocative efficiency)	• Firms have some price making power • Normal profit for all firms in long run (but short run losses or supernormal profit are possible) • Production not at minimum AC and P does not equal MC	• Outcomes depend on the strategies adopted by firms • Firms may collude or compete on price • Branding and non-price competition are common features	• Price making powers are used by the firm to restrict quantity and raise price • Long run supernormal profit • A lack of productive efficiency (production not at minimum AC) and lack of allocative efficiency (P does not equal MC)

Contestable markets theory argues that market concentration is less important than the threat of new competition in influencing the conduct of incumbent firms. Typical behaviour in a market without entry or exit barriers includes entry-limit pricing, building artificial entry barriers and the possibility of 'hit and run' competition. Highly contestable markets tend to produce broadly efficient outcomes.

Chapter
16

Unit 4: Measuring the macroeconomy → How the macroeconomy works →
Macroeconomic performance → Macroeconomic policy tools → International Economics

Living Standards, Development and Sustainability

National income and living standards

It is common to use national income as an indicator of a country's living standards. **GDP per capita** (GDP divided by population) is the most frequently used variable. However, it should be noted that GDP per capita figures are only an indication of **material living standards** and tell us nothing about the non-material aspects of quality of life. Even comparing material living standards is difficult.

GDP per capita figures may not give an accurate comparison even of material living standards

Difficulties in using GDP per capita figures to measure material living standards include:

● **The figures take no account of the distribution of income.** The income of a country with a high GDP per capita figure may be concentrated in the hands of small section of the population, with the rest of the population being poor. This tends to be the case in oil rich countries. There are significant pockets of poverty in the UK, despite our high per capita GDP. The degree of inequality can be examined using the concepts of the **Lorenz Curve** and **Gini coefficient** (see Chapter 15).

● **GDP figures understate national income because they do not include black market activity.** Such unrecorded activity would significantly boost the recorded national income if it was included.

● **GDP figures understate national income because they do not include the value of non-traded output.** We all produce valuable economic output that we do not trade. If households paid someone else to do all their washing, ironing, cooking, cleaning, decorating and other maintenance currently undertaken on a do-it-yourself basis, this would add to national income. In developing countries, subsistence agriculture (families growing crops for consumption rather than trade) means that GDP figures significantly underestimate income.

● **Price changes can make it difficult to compare GDP per capita over time.** This means that GDP per capita figures should be adjusted for inflation to give **real** GDP per capita.

● **It is necessary to convert GDP per capita figures into a common currency in order to make international comparisons possible.** The American dollar is often used for this purpose.

● **The choice of the exchange rate for making the conversion to a common currency crucially affects the outcome.** Converting the UK GDP per capita at £1 = $1.80 instead of £1 = $1.50 would give a 20% higher per capita income in dollars. The correct exchange rate to use is the **purchasing power parity** (**PPP**) exchange rate, which adjusts for price differentials between countries. PPP exchange rates give the same purchasing power for any given sum of money when it is converted into another currency. The GDP per capita of developing countries tends to be higher when using purchasing power parity rates for conversion than when using market exchange rates. This is because any given sum of money has greater purchasing power in developing countries due to the low price levels in these countries.

● **International comparisons can be difficult due to differences in accounting procedures and the accuracy of GDP statistics collected in different countries.**

Non-material aspects of standard of living

There is clearly more to a good standard of living than how many goods and services a society is able to produce and consume. A more complete picture would take into account a variety of other factors. These might include:

● **Environmental indicators** such as air quality, water quality, greenhouse gas emissions, access to green space and areas of outstanding natural beauty, biodiversity (number of different species of plants and wildlife, for example), etc.

● **Social indicators** such as crime rates, divorce rates and quality of human relationships (although this is very difficult to measure). 'Work life balance' has become a particular issue in developed nations.

● **Educational indicators** such as literacy and numeracy rates and the percentage of the relevant age group enrolled in primary, secondary and higher education. The rate of primary school enrolment is particularly important in developing countries.

● **Health indicators** such as life expectancy and infant mortality rates and indicators relating to particular illnesses such as heart disease. The incidence of depression and stress related illnesses also receives particular attention in developed nations.

● **Political freedoms** such as the right to vote and free speech.

Economic growth and development

The economist Michael Todaro has identified three objectives of economic development. These are:

● **To increase the availability and widen the distribution of basic life sustaining goods.** This relates to the provision of the basic human needs (food, drink, clothing, warmth, shelter and sanitation).

● **To raise standards of living.** This may primarily mean material living standards, but consideration should also be given to non-material factors, amongst which Todaro identifies self-esteem as especially important.

● **To expand the range of economic and social choices.** This objective should be taken to include political freedoms.

Development economics tends to focus on the alleviation of **absolute poverty** where basic needs are not met. Absolute poverty is measured by the World Bank using income thresholds of either $1 or $2 per day.

Development and growth are linked. Even if the immediate benefits of growth are unequally distributed, there may be '**trickle down effects**' as spending by the wealthy creates employment opportunities for others. However, experience suggests that absolute poverty can affect many individuals even in a society where national income is high. The International Monetary Fund promotes 'high quality growth'. This is defined as growth that is sustainable, and brings lasting gains in employment and living standards.

Sustainable development

Sustainable development is development that does not compromise the quality of life for future generations. This concept has been given more weight as it becomes apparent that human economic activity is causing significant environmental problems (see material on resource depletion and resource degradation in Chapter 11). Of particular concern is the emission of greenhouse gases, which scientific research indicates is contributing to global warming.

Alternative measures of growth and development: (1) The UN's Human Development Index (HDI) and Human Poverty Index (HPI)

The **Human Development Index** (HDI) is a summary index that measures three aspects of human development namely: longevity (life expectancy), knowledge (adult literacy rate) and a decent standard of living (GDP per capita). It is clearly possible for countries with similar incomes to have very different levels of human development, as suggested by Figure 16.1.

Development economics tends to focus on the alleviation of absolute poverty.

Figure 16.1

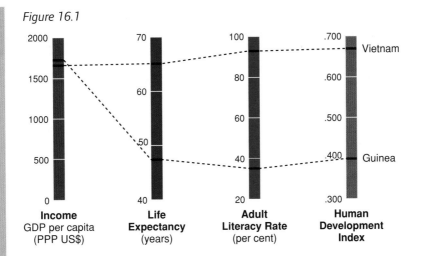

Income	**Life**	**Adult**	**Human**
GDP per capita	**Expectancy**	**Literacy Rate**	**Development**
(PPP US$)	(years)	(per cent)	**Index**

The **Human Poverty Index** (HPI) is constructed in the same way as the HDI. It too includes measures of longevity, knowledge and decent standards of living, but uses indicators that focus on deprivation (e.g. the probability of not surviving to a certain age rather than life expectancy). Two HPI measures are published, one for developing countries and one for developed countries.

The HDI and HPI measures are summarised in the following table:

Index	Longevity	Knowledge	Decent standard of living	Participation or exclusion
HDI	Life expectancy at birth	1. Adult literacy rate 2. Combined enrolment ratio	GDP per capita (PPP US$)	Not applicable
HPI-1 (developing countries)	Probability at birth of not surviving until age 40	Adult illiteracy rate	Deprivation measured by: 1. Percentage of people not using improved water sources 2. Percentage of children under 5 who are underweight	Not applicable
HPI-2 (developed countries)	Probability at birth of not surviving to age 60	Percentage of adults lacking functional literacy skills	Percentage of people living below the poverty line (50% of median disposable household income)	Long-term unemployment rate (12 months or more)

Source: UN Human Development Report 2001

(2) The Index of Sustainable Economic Welfare (ISEW)

The Index of Sustainable Economic Welfare (ISEW) is promoted as an alternative to measuring living standards using solely GDP. The following definition of ISEW comes from 'Friends of the Earth': "It is an attempt to measure the part of economic activity that genuinely increases the quality of life. For example, it makes a subtraction for air pollution caused by economic activity, and makes an addition to count unpaid household labour – such as cleaning or child minding. It also covers areas such as income inequality, other environmental damage, and depletion of environmental assets."

The ISEW is a highly controversial indicator. For example, it has been criticised for introducing subjective measures of the value of environmental damage, and the weighting that should be attached to income inequality, to produce what some people will misinterpret as an objective economic indicator.

Chapter
17

Unit 4: Measuring the macroeconomy → **How the macroeconomy works** →
Macroeconomic performance → Macroeconomic policy tools → International Economics

Economic Growth and the Business Cycle

Economic growth

Economic growth is measured as the year on year increase in real GDP and can be defined as an increase in the productive potential of the economy.

Short run (current or actual) economic growth can occur as a result of an increase in aggregate demand, where AD = C + I + G + (X - M). An increase in aggregate demand brings **spare capacity** into use as the **derived demand** for factors of production increases. The **output gap** closes and the economy moves closer to its productive potential.

Note that an initial increase in AD may create **multiplier effects** that lead to a larger increase in GDP. Another way of looking at this is that it takes the economy closer to its **production possibility frontier**. Such growth is *not* sustainable and will be brought to an end once the economy has no more spare capacity. At this point, further increases in aggregate demand would be purely inflationary. This can be illustrated using an AS/AD diagram such as Figure A2.5 from Appendix 2.

Long run economic growth requires an increase in the productive potential of the economy. This could be the result of an increase in the quantity and quality of land, labour, capital and enterprise available and comes from the supply side of the economy. This can be illustrated using an AS/AD diagram such as Figure A2.7 or Figure A2.10 from Appendix 2. Long run growth can also be shown as an outwards shift of a PPF.

Trend growth

Trend growth (the underlying rate of growth) can be defined in the following ways:

● It is the long run average growth rate of an economy (over at least one complete business cycle).

● It is the growth rate that the economy can sustain without generating inflationary pressure.

An economy's trend growth rate is determined by the rate of growth of its protective potential. For example, a trend growth rate of 2.5% suggests that on average the capacity of the economy grows at 2.5% per annum. Remember that an economy's productive potential is a function of the quantity and quality (productivity) of the factors of production (land, labour, capital and enterprise) available.

The business cycle

The cycle describes the pattern of GDP as it fluctuates around trend growth, which is shown as the best-fit line in Figure 17.1. Typical characteristics of each stage include:

Recovery (Point B onwards) – Rising output, falling unemployment, increased inflationary pressure and a deteriorating balance of payments are associated with the recovery phase of the economic cycle.

Recession (Point A to B) – Broadly speaking, the reverse of the above. A recession is defined as at least two successive quarters of falling GDP. This phase of the economic cycle is associated with falling output, rising unemployment, reduced inflationary pressure and improvements in the balance of payments.

Peaks (Point A) and **troughs** (Point B) – These are points at which output is higher or lower than in the surrounding years.

Booms are periods of strong output growth, above the trend rate. They are likely to be associated with a tight labour market and accelerating wage settlements. It is likely that inflation will accelerate as the growth of AD outstrips that of AS.

Slowdowns occur when the pace of output growth slows without actually falling.

Figure 17.1: The business cycle

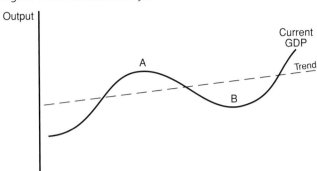

If the economy grows faster than **trend** for any significant period of time, this suggests aggregate demand is growing faster than productive potential. This is likely to reduce unemployment, but may be inflationary as the **output gap** closes. There may even be a positive output gap, with the economy temporarily operating beyond full capacity (for example, through overtime work). See Figure 17.2.

Below trend growth suggests demand is growing at a slower rate than productive potential. The output gap grows and so too does unemployment, but inflationary pressure will be reduced.

If the economy grows at its trend rate, no inflationary pressure is generated and there is a greater chance of economic stability. The trend rate of growth is seen as the sustainable growth rate for the economy.

Figure 17.2: The output gap over the business cycle

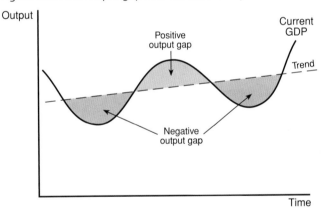

Given that trend growth is determined by the rate at which productive potential increases, we need to look at the influences on the quantity and quality of factors of production to find out what determines trend growth.

The influences on trend growth

Economies with high trend growth rates tend to:

- **Invest** a substantial proportion of their GDP, thus boosting the quantity and quality of their capital stock.

- Devote resources to research & development in order to achieve **technological advances** (although it is also possible to receive external benefits from the technological advances made by other countries).

- Have high quality education and training systems, raising the **productivity** of workers.

- Have '**flexible labour markets**' with workers willing to adapt to new working practices, thereby enhancing their productivity.

● Benefit from a strong **entrepreneurial culture**, perhaps supported by a policy framework of low corporate taxes and only light regulation by the government.

● Possess a **strong institutional structure**. This might imply adequate protection of property rights, including patents for 'intellectual property' such as new ideas. There should also be a strong financial system to provide the finance that firms need in order to invest and innovate.

Costs and benefits of growth

Economic growth leads to the following benefits:

1. Higher economic growth should lead to an increase in **living standards** as measured by real GDP per capita.

2. The effects of growth are cumulative. If a country grows at 3% per annum, the economy will double in size every 24 years. Growth helps make future investment more affordable.

3. Economic growth should reduce **unemployment**. When output in the economy increases there should be an increase in the demand for labour. This is because labour is a **derived demand**, that is to say that the demand for labour is dependent on the final demand for goods and services. Firms do not demand labour for its own sake.

4. Economic growth will **automatically** have a positive effect on government finances. Economic growth will increase tax revenues because as output, employment and incomes rise so will the tax take. Growth will reduce unemployment and, as a result, expenditure on **transfer payments** will fall. See Chapter 19 for more details.

5. Rising demand and output encourages further investment in new capital machinery via the **accelerator process**. This will boost the productive capacity of the economy in the long run.

Economic growth encourages further investment in new capital machinery via the accelerator process.

Economic growth leads to the following costs:

1. Economic growth creates **negative externalities**, such as increased pollution and congestion, which damage social welfare. Those affected could experience a fall in living standards.

2. The benefits of economic growth may not be evenly distributed. A rise in national output may also be associated with growing inequality in society. Just because there is economic growth, it does not mean that the number of people living in absolute poverty will diminish.

3. Faster economic growth might lead to an over exploitation of scarce finite economic resources (resource depletion) that will limit growth prospects in the future.

4. If current growth exceeds trend growth there is a danger of **inflation**. The rise in prices may reduce the **international competitiveness** of the economy.

Why is there a business cycle?

When the level of output is increasing/decreasing, there are forces at work that help keep the movement going in the same direction. The interaction of **multiplier** and **accelerator** effects helps keep the level of AD increasing or decreasing. To understand why there is a business cycle, we now need to understand what causes turning points.

External shocks

One explanation of the turning points in the business cycle is provided by the possibility of **external shocks**. These may come from government policy interventions or from events in other economies. The impact of shocks from other countries has increased in recent years as economies have become more interconnected or 'globalised'.

External shocks can originate from both the supply side and demand side of the economy.

Perhaps the most likely **supply side shock** is a sudden increase in the price of oil. This raises the cost of production and reduces short run aggregate supply (see Figure A2.8 in Appendix 2). This may simultaneously reduce output and create inflation.

A tightening of monetary or fiscal policy (to tackle inflation) could be seen as a **demand shock**, as could a recession in a country that is a key export market. In 2008, a financial crisis raised the cost of credit, restricted aggregate demand and caused a global recession.

Endogenous explanations of turning points: Ceilings and floors

The term 'endogenous' refers to factors that are internal to the workings of the economic system. They may create a **ceiling** to stop the economy growing: There is a physical limit to the availability of factors of production, preventing indefinite growth. Similarly there is likely to be a **floor** to stop output falling: a recession will never see output fall to zero. This is because consumers must sustain a basic level of consumption to survive and worn out capital must eventually be replaced.

Chapter

18

Unit 4: Measuring the macroeconomy → **How the macroeconomy works** →
Macroeconomic performance → Macroeconomic policy tools → International Economics

Unemployment, Inflation and Deflation

Unemployment

The unemployed are those individuals of working age who are actively seeking work but do not have a job. Unemployment can be measured in two ways:

- **The claimant count** measure of unemployment simply counts the numbers claiming unemployment related benefit on a given day each month.

- The **Labour Force Survey (LFS) method** is based on a monthly survey of 6000 households and uses the **International Labour Organisation (ILO)** definition of unemployment. It covers those who have looked for work in the past four weeks and are available to start work in the next two weeks.

More detail on the problems of measuring unemployment can be found in the AS Revision Guide.

Causes of unemployment

Unemployment can result from a lack of demand (**demand deficient unemployment**) or various problems on the **supply side** of the economy (real wage unemployment, frictional unemployment and structural unemployment).

Demand deficient unemployment

Demand deficient unemployment is associated with an economic recession. It is a form of **disequilibrium** unemployment as there is not enough demand to generate a job for all those wishing to work at current wage rates. Labour is a **derived demand** – it is not demanded for its own sake, but because of the output that it produces. As aggregate demand drops, firms will lay off workers to reduce their costs and protect profits.

Figure 18.1: Demand deficient unemployment

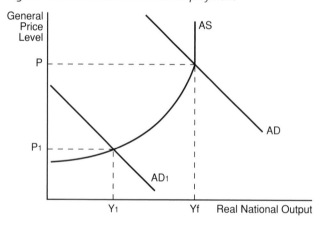

In Figure 18.1, the equilibrium level of national output (Y1) lies below the full employment level of national output (Yf). This means that there is insufficient aggregate demand for all workers to obtain employment. The current level of demand (AD1) lies below the level required for full employment (AD).

Although demand deficient unemployment is usually associated with economic recessions it can also exist in the long run when the economy has an **output gap**. This occurs when actual output lies below potential output.

Real wage unemployment

Real wage unemployment is a form of **disequilibrium unemployment** that occurs when **real wages** are forced above **the market clearing level**. Traditionally, **trade unions** and **minimum wage legislation** have been seen as the main cause of this type of unemployment.

Suppose that having initially been in equilibrium where the demand for labour was equal to the supply of labour, a minimum wage W1 is set above the market clearing wage W. The effects of such an action are illustrated in Figure 18.2.

Figure 18.2: Classical unemployment

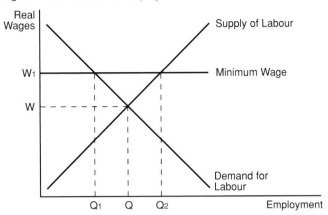

At the new minimum wage W1, the **demand for labour** has contracted from Q to Q1 while the supply of labour has expanded from Q to Q2. Firms will tend to employ fewer workers when the marginal cost of employing them increases. At the same time, more workers will be willing to take jobs at higher wage rates.

At real wage W1, there is an **excess supply of labour**. The supply of labour now exceeds the demand for labour and we have disequilibrium unemployment equal to Q2-Q1.

We are assuming that a rise in real wages does not cause a rise in productivity or consumer expenditure. If productivity, and/or consumption, did increase then the demand for labour would shift to the right and the rise in unemployment would be far smaller.

Equilibrium unemployment

Equilibrium unemployment is unemployment that can exist even when the demand for labour is equal to the supply of labour. The are two types of equilibrium unemployment: frictional and structural

Frictional unemployment

This type of unemployment reflects job turnover in the labour market. Even when there are vacancies it takes people time to search and find a new job. During this period of time workers will remain frictionally unemployed.

Structural unemployment

Structural unemployment occurs when there is a mismatch between the characteristics of the unemployed and the characteristics needed in order to fill the vacancies in an economy.

Structural unemployment is caused by immobility of labour:

● Occupational immobility is associated with a lack of transferable skills, preventing workers from moving from one job to another.

● Geographical immobility prevents workers moving from one area to another in order to fill vacancies.

Inflation

Inflation is a persistent increase in the general level of prices over time.

The main measures of inflation are the Retail Price Index (RPI) and, the government's preferred measure, the Consumer Price Index (CPI). More detail on the measurement of inflation can be found in the AS Revision Guide.

Causes of inflation

There are two main causes of inflation: demand pull and cost push.

Demand pull inflation

Demand pull inflation occurs when total demand for goods and services exceeds total supply. This type of inflation happens when there has been **excessive growth in aggregate demand** or when **current growth exceeds trend growth**.

Figure 18.3: Demand pull inflation

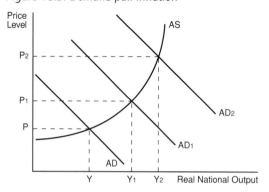

- At low levels of output when there is plenty of spare productive capacity (a substantial output gap), firms can easily expand output to meet increases in demand, resulting in a relatively elastic AS curve (see the shift from AD to AD1, giving only moderate inflation of P to P1).

- However, as the economy approaches full capacity and the output gap closes, labour and raw material shortages mean that it becomes more difficult for firms to expand production without pushing up their prices (see the shift from AD1 to AD2, giving more substantial inflation from P1 to P2).

- At the same time, many firms will choose to widen their profit margins. As a result, prices will rise sharply. It is likely that, as employment in the economy grows, demand for goods and services will become more inelastic. This will allow firms to pass on large price increases without any significant contraction in demand.

Cost push inflation

This occurs when firms increase prices to maintain or protect profit margins after experiencing a rise in costs. The main causes are:

- Growth in **Unit Labour Costs** – this occurs when average wages grow faster than productivity.

- Rising **input** costs – such as oil, raw materials and components.

- Increases in **indirect taxes** – VAT and excise duties are paid by producers and will, therefore, increase their costs.

- Higher **import prices** – a depreciation in the currency, or a rise in world inflation rates, will force up import prices.

The effects of a rise in costs are illustrated in Figure 18.4.

Figure 18.4: Cost push inflation

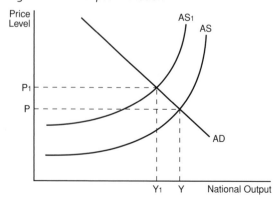

An increase in **input costs** will mean that firms can produce less at each and every price level and, as a result, the aggregate supply curve will shift to the left from AS to AS1.

● At the new equilibrium level of national output, the economy is producing a lower level of output Y1 at a higher price level P1. Higher cost push inflation therefore causes a contraction in real output as well as a higher price level.

● However, increases in the costs of firms do not always feed through to inflation. Firms may choose to absorb the increase in costs and accept reduced profit margins on each unit sold, especially when the consumer is very sensitive to price increases as may be the case during, and immediately after, a recession.

The opening section of this chapter revises the basic measurement and causes of both unemployment and inflation. It is also important to have an appreciation of the costs of unemployment and inflation.

A more comprehensive treatment of the following summary table can be found in the AS Revision Guide.

Costs of unemployment	Costs of inflation
Lost output. Unemployment causes a waste of scarce resources and reduces the growth potential of the economy. The economy operates inside its production possibility frontier and has spare capacity (an output gap).	**Inefficient resource allocation.** Volatile inflation results in lack of information about relative prices. The price mechanism is affected.
Impact on government finances. An increase in unemployment results in higher benefit payments and lower direct tax revenues, as the unemployed pay no income tax. Because they also spend less, indirect tax revenues are reduced too.	**Disruption of business planning.** Unpredictable inflation may reduce investment and therefore limit growth. **Reduced competitiveness** in international trade if prices rise faster than in other countries. **A wage-price spiral** is likely if higher inflation raises inflationary expectations that feed into wage bargaining.
Training resources are wasted, as the unemployed do not use their skills. They may also become deskilled as their skills become increasingly dated in a rapidly changing labour market.	**The real value of savings is reduced** (as is the real value of debt). Inflation favours borrowers at the expense of savers. **The real value of fixed incomes is reduced** (e.g. affecting those with pensions that are not index linked).
Rising unemployment is linked to social and economic deprivation. There appears to be a relationship between unemployment and crime and social dislocation (increased divorce rates, worsening health and lower life expectancy).	**Shoe leather costs.** Inflation increases time taken to make price comparisons and making trips to banks as the opportunity cost of holding money increases. **Menu costs.** These are the costs to firms of changing price information.

The natural rate of unemployment

The natural rate of unemployment (NRU) can be defined in a number of different ways. However, at A2 level the NRU can be seen as the rate of unemployment an economy experiences when the **labour market is in equilibrium**. At this point, only frictional and structural unemployment remain. Frictional and structural unemployment can exist even when there is at least one vacancy in the economy for every unemployed worker (so that total labour demand at least matches labour supply). The problem is that the unemployed are not able to fill the vacancies. Figure 18.5 illustrates the natural rate of unemployment. Those who are frictionally and structurally unemployed are part of the labour force but are not an effective part of the labour supply. The natural rate can be seen as the quantity of voluntary unemployment (ab) expressed as a percentage of the labour force.

Figure 18.5: The natural rate of unemployment

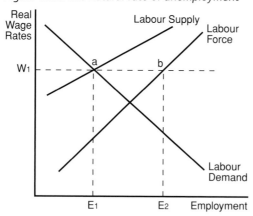

Some economists also view the NRU as a modern definition of **full employment**. It is not realistic to have every member of the workforce in a job. Increases in aggregate demand will never be able to achieve full employment because of the existence of supply side imperfections in the labour market.

The NRU is difficult to measure but can be seen as the **long term trend path of unemployment** (determined by the supply side performance of the economy), while the current level of unemployment fluctuates around the long term trend due to fluctuations in the level of aggregate demand.

The non-accelerating inflation rate of unemployment (NAIRU)

The **non-accelerating inflation rate of unemployment** (**NAIRU**) is the level of unemployment compatible with maintaining a stable inflation rate.

At any given time, there will be an anticipated inflation rate embedded in the minds of economic agents. This rate is influenced by **inflationary expectations**. The Bank of England has worked hard to establish the **credibility** of the 2% inflation target. If firms and workers believe that the inflation rate will stay at 2%, this influences wage negotiations and makes it more likely that this rate will be achieved.

Should unemployment be driven below the NRU by increases in aggregate demand, it is likely that inflation will accelerate because labour demand will now exceed labour supply. This 'tight' labour market is likely to put upward pressure on wage claims and cause a rise in inflation: unemployment below the natural rate is not compatible with maintaining a stable inflation rate.

The Phillips Curve

The **Phillips Curve** is a graphical representation of the relationship between unemployment and inflation. This is shown in Figure 18.6(a). It suggests that a **short run trade off** between unemployment and inflation exists (higher AD is likely to reduce unemployment, but may generate inflationary pressure). If unemployment is driven below the NAIRU, the resulting increase in inflation is especially sharp.

The Phillips Curve trade off helps us to understand the results of changes in AD, but does not accurately depict the result of changes in aggregate supply. A fall in aggregate supply, for example, can cause inflation and unemployment to rise simultaneously.

To understand the long term relationship between unemployment and inflation, it is helpful to study the **expectations augmented Phillips Curve**. In Figure 18.6(b), suppose that inflation is low and stable at 2%, with unemployment at the NAIRU. The economy is in long run equilibrium.

An increase in AD then pushes unemployment down, but inflation will rise to 4%. The economy is now at Point B. If the new 4% inflation rate becomes built into expectations and wage settlements begin to reflect this, the short run aggregate supply will shift left and, as a result, unemployment will rise as workers are laid off. Unemployment has returned to the NAIRU, but inflation of 4% is now embedded in the economy. The economy has now moved to Point C.

The initial boost in AD has had no long term impact on unemployment and there is no long run trade off between inflation and unemployment. The short run trade off is now centred on the new higher inflation rate (see SRPC2).

This theory suggests that supply side factors are the most important determinants of unemployment in the long run. A further implication of the Phillips Curve model is that to keep inflation low it is important that the government has a **credible** counter inflation policy that is successful in anchoring down inflationary expectations.

Figure 18.6

| (a) The original Phillips Curve | (b) The expectations augmented Phillips Curve |

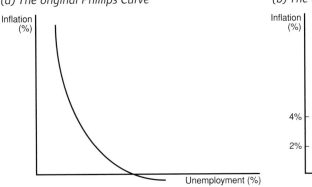
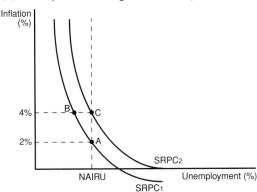

The key policy implications of the expectations augmented Phillips Curve are that:

● If unemployment is below the NAIRU, then inflation will accelerate. If this situation persists for any length of time, it is likely that higher inflationary expectations will be embedded in the economy.

● If unemployment is higher than the NAIRU, then inflation is likely to fall. Again this can permanently affect inflation if inflationary expectations adjust to the new lower rate.

Policies to reduce unemployment

To reduce unemployment, it is important to use a policy that is appropriate to the type of unemployment that is causing the problem. The AS Revision Guide looked at the policy measures that can be used to tackle the various types of unemployment. The focus of this section will be to evaluate the problems associated with these different policies.

Demand side policies

If a recession, or below trend growth, has generated demand deficient unemployment, an **expansionary fiscal** or **monetary policy** may be the appropriate policy response. The aim of these policies is to stimulate AD so that the **derived demand** for labour increases, enabling the **output gap** to be closed as **spare capacity** is reduced. There are, however, problems when using such policies:

● The size of the stimulus that is needed depends on the size of the **output gap**. It is important to be aware that the output gap is difficult to measure, so it may be difficult to assess the size of the fiscal or monetary stimulus required because of a **lack of information**.

● Similarly, it is difficult to judge the size of the **multiplier**. Suppose a government wants to increase national output by £1,000m to reduce unemployment. The government cannot calculate the required increase in expenditure without knowing the exact value of the multiplier. Suppose the multiplier is estimated to be 2, the government would increase spending by £500m. If, however, this estimate was wrong and the multiplier was 3, national output would increase by £1,500m and an inflation problem might be created. The multiplier is changing all the time as withdrawals in the economy fluctuate and, as a result, government policies may not always achieve their desired goal. This makes it very difficult for the government to **control** and **fine tune** the economy.

● It is also important to note that fiscal and monetary policy suffers from **time lags**. Given such difficulties it would be easy to over stimulate the economy and generate inflation, so it is important that the government exercises caution.

Supply side policies

To achieve permanent reductions in unemployment, it is necessary to tackle the supply side causes of unemployment, in an effort to reduce the **NAIRU**. Broadly speaking, this implies policies that will make the labour market more flexible and tackle frictional and structural unemployment.

Flexible labour markets

A flexible labour market is one in which labour supply is highly responsive to labour demand. The key aspects of labour market flexibility are:

● **Labour mobility.** Workers possess transferable skills, or the ability to acquire new ones, and this enhances occupational mobility. If workers are willing to move from region to region this will improve the geographical mobility of labour.

● **Flexible working patterns** (such as part-time work, variable hours contracts, shift work and temporary contracts) reduce the costs to firms of taking on workers because firms can vary the hours of work in response to changing economic conditions without having to pay overtime or redundancy payments.

● **Wage flexibility.** Wages should be flexible both upwards and downwards in response to changing labour market conditions, so that the wage can act as a signal that allocates labour resources efficiently. This implies a need for local pay bargaining. Wages for a whole profession (e.g. teachers) should not be set at a national level.

Policies to tackle frictional unemployment

Policies to tackle frictional unemployment include:

● **Reducing Job Seeker's Allowance** (formerly unemployment benefit) – the job seeker has to show that he/she is **actively seeking work** and if they are unable to prove this at fortnightly interviews they lose their benefit. This measure was introduced to reduce the level of frictional unemployment. However, if the government reduced the level of the benefit, or limited the duration of a claim, search time between jobs could be reduced even further. This is because workers would have to take a job more quickly before their financial situations deteriorated. Some economists argue that if the unemployed were financially worse off they would not be able to search for work effectively. For example, they may not be able to afford to travel to interviews or telephone potential employers.

● **Direct tax cuts** – the government could reduce direct taxes for the low paid to increase the post tax wage and, therefore, encourage them to find work more quickly. Most analysts believe that tax cuts on their own are insufficient to reduce frictional unemployment. The benefit system needs to be reformed to eliminate the **unemployment trap** – this is a situation where someone is financially better off not working.

● **Improving job information** – facilities provided by job centres, private agencies, newspapers and the Internet. The development of the Job Centre Plus programme, which provides intensive support and advice for job seekers, is one way to help workers obtain employment more quickly.

| **Policies to tackle structural unemploy- ment** | Policies to tackle structural unemployment include: |

- **Regional policy** – involves giving grants and tax breaks to encourage firms to locate in areas of high structural unemployment. This, however, does not solve the problem of **occupational immobility**. Regional policy often demands extra retraining schemes in order to give workers the relevant skills to allow them to take up new jobs.

- **Investment in worker training** – The **New Deal** programme aims to provide a gateway back into employment for long term unemployed workers. The scheme starts with an interview to identify any gaps in a worker's skills, training or knowledge. An individual programme is then developed for each participant. The options available within the programme include: subsidised employment; work experience with employers; training and help with basic skills; a place on an environmental taskforce. The aim of the scheme is to give workers the training and skills needed to take up jobs in their local areas. It is also hoped that real work experience will improve their employability.

- **Improving geographical mobility** – the government could provide grants or low cost housing to encourage workers to move from areas of high unemployment to regions where there are jobs. The problem with this policy is that people are inherently immobile because they are often bound by family and social ties.

- **The market solution** – one approach is simply to leave the problem of structural unemployment to the market. High unemployment will drive down wages and new firms will be attracted into a region to take advantage of the low costs of production. In this way the problem will eventually solve itself, but the **social deprivation** created in the short term may be considerable. Some commentators argue that intervention to solve structural unemployment slows the natural reallocation of resources to high growth areas and only makes the problem worse.

Policies that tackle frictional and structural unemployment will reduce the NAIRU and make the short run trade-off between inflation and unemployment more favourable, so that the points on the current short run Phillips Curve represent low unemployment/low inflation combinations.

| **Policies to tackle inflation** | Demand side management of inflation tends to focus on monetary policy. This will be covered in Chapter 20. The flexible labour market policies outlined to tackle frictional and structural unemployment will also help to reduce cost push inflationary pressures. More detail on other policies to tackle inflation can be found in the AS Revision Guide. |

| **Deflation** | It is important to be aware that the general price level can fall. This is called deflation and should be distinguished from a situation where prices rise, but merely at a slower rate. Deflation has been unusual in modern times, but it became a reality in 2009. |

Deflation is arguably more damaging than inflation because it creates an incentive to defer expenditure, as consumers and firms wait for prices to fall further. This lack of demand can lead to substantial falls in GDP. A further problem is that deflation increases the **real value of debt**, and increases the likelihood of both consumer and firms defaulting on debts.

Chapter

19

Unit 4: Measuring the macroeconomy → How the macroeconomy works →
Macroeconomic performance → **Macroeconomic policy tools** → International Economics

Fiscal Policy

Fiscal policy

Fiscal policy involves the use of **government expenditure** and **taxation** to influence the level and composition of aggregate demand.

Contractionary policy involves cutting government spending or raising taxes	**Expansionary policy** involves raising government spending or cutting taxes
Budget surplus: tax revenue > government expenditure	Budget deficit: government expenditure > tax revenue
Government provides net leakages from the circular flow	Government provides a net injection to the circular flow
AD falls and economic activity contracts	AD rises and economic activity expands

Some key terms relating to fiscal policy

It is important to be able to define the following keys terms:

● The **public sector** is simply the government sector of the economy.

● The government's **budget** refers to the relative levels of government spending and tax revenue over a year.

● The **public sector net cash requirement** (PSNCR) is the amount the government needs to borrow each year. It is also called a budget deficit. It is equal to government expenditure minus tax revenue.

● Government spending can be divided into **current spending** (e.g. teachers' wages) and **capital spending** (e.g. building a school).

● Taxation revenues come from **direct taxes** levied on income, wealth and profit (e.g. income tax and corporation tax) and **indirect taxes** levied on expenditure (e.g. VAT and specific unit duties).

Refer back to the AS Revision Guide to look at some of the other key terms that are crucial to understanding fiscal policy.

The uses of fiscal policy

Fiscal policy can be used to achieve a number of economic objectives:

● **Managing the level of AD.** For example, during a recession the government may wish to **introduce an expansionary fiscal policy**. This can be achieved by an increase in government expenditure, or a cut in taxes, to **stimulate economic growth** and **generate employment**. This helps to close large output gaps (see Figure A2.5 in Appendix 2).

● **Influencing the pattern of AD.** Governments may wish to allocate more resources to public goods (such as street lighting) and merit goods (such as education and activities). This can be achieved by the state providing public goods and subsidising the consumption of merit goods. It might also be desirable to allocate fewer resources towards demerit goods, such as cigarettes. This explains why cigarettes are taxed so heavily. Taxes and subsidies can be used to affect the pattern of AD and to tackle market failures.

● **Redistributing income.** Governments often operate a progressive tax system (taking a higher proportion of income from higher income earners) and provide benefits to those on low incomes. Such policies narrow the distribution of income.

● **Paying for essential government services.** There are some services, such as the regulation of economic activity, that must be financed.

Automatic and discretionary fiscal policy

Figure 19.1: The public sector net cash requirement

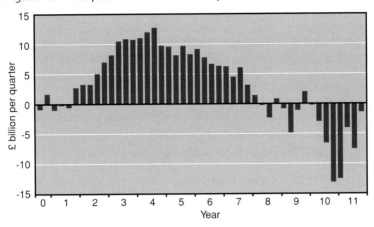

In Figure 19.1, the government runs a budget deficit (government expenditure exceeds tax revenue) from Year 1 to Year 7, with the size of that deficit peaking at around £12 billion a quarter in Year 4.

There are two possible reasons for such an occurrence.

Automatic stabilisers

● **Automatic stabilisers** describe how government expenditure and tax revenues respond to changes in the economic cycle. There is no deliberate change in policy, but the amount of money the government spends and receives will fluctuate with the economic cycle. A budget deficit automatically increases in a recession. This is because higher unemployment stimulates benefit expenditure and, at the same time, tax revenues fall due to lower consumer spending and shrinking incomes. These changes help **stabilise** the economy and **reduce the magnitude** of the recession.

Discretionary policy

● **Discretionary policy** refers to the deliberate manipulation of government expenditure levels and tax rates. For example, during a recession the government may decide to spend more money or to cut tax rates in order to stimulate the economy. It may at any time decide to increase discretionary spending to improve public services, such as healthcare and education. Discretionary policy changes provide another possible explanation for the growing budget deficit from Years 1 to 4.

Cyclical and structural deficits

A **cyclical budget deficit** is a temporary phenomenon that occurs during a recession, or a slowdown of the rate of economic growth. The impact of automatic stabilisers means that the government needs to borrow to bridge the gap between government spending and tax revenue. However, this will be balanced by a budget surplus later on in the economic cycle when the economy is growing more strongly.

A **structural deficit** persists regardless of the stage of the business cycle. It is likely to increase during a recession and fall during recovery, but remains present at all times. Running a structural budget deficit is likely to be unsustainable because it implies the need for the government to find new sources for funds.

Should governments run budget deficits? (evaluation)

Most economists would argue that a persistently large budget deficit can be a major problem for the government and the economy. This is because:

● A PSNCR has to be **financed**. This is done by issuing **government debt** to domestic or overseas investors. In some circumstances, interest rates may have to be raised to attract investors to buy the debt. This may lead to **crowding out** of private sector activity. Higher interest rates will **reduce economic growth** and **create unemployment**. At the same time if the public sector is growing it may deprive the private sector of much needed skilled labour and restrict the growth of private firms.

● In the **long run**, a high PSNCR adds to the accumulated **National Debt**. This means that the Government has to pay more each year in **debt interest charges**. The **opportunity cost** of debt interest is that the money could be used in more productive ways, such as spending on education or health. Debt interest also represents a **transfer of income** from tax payers to those who hold government debt. A high PSNCR may, therefore, cause a redistribution of income and wealth in the economy.

● **'Today's borrowing is tomorrow's taxes'.** At some point in the future a budget deficit has to be reduced. The government could cut back on spending, but normally it chooses to increase **taxes**.

A budget deficit may not be a problem in certain circumstances:

● Keynesian economists argue that a PSNCR is a vital **stimulus to demand** when the economy is in a recession. A budget deficit automatically increases in a recession. These changes help stabilise the economy and **reduce the magnitude** of the recession.

● If a PSNCR is used to finance **capital spending** it may improve the performance of the economy in the long run. Spending on new infrastructure **increases the productive potential** of the economy and shifts the AS curve to the right. This may allow the economy to achieve a faster rate of growth in the future and this will generate higher tax revenues to pay for the borrowing. The current government believes that public sector borrowing should only be used to finance capital projects over the course of an economic cycle. This is known as the 'golden rule' and implies that a budget deficit should never be used to fund welfare spending. This ensures that the PSNCR never spirals out of control and that borrowing always boosts the **supply side capacity** of the economy.

Problems with fiscal policy

There are a number of general problems that might occur if the government uses fiscal policy:

● There are **informational problems**. The government needs to know the size of the output gap and the multiplier.

● **Time lags.** More detail on these problems can be found in Chapter 18. However, it appears that the government should proceed with caution if making a discretionary choice to stimulate the economy. It is very difficult to fine tune the economy.

What is a good tax?

Adam Smith suggested that a good tax should be:

● **Certain** – The timing and the size of the tax burden should be clearly known to the taxpayer.

● **Convenient** – It should be easy for the taxpayer to make a tax payment.

● **Cheap to collect** – The cost of collecting the tax is a low percentage of the revenue yielded.

● **Equitable** – The amount paid should be fair (it should be related to the ability to pay).

To this list of points a modern economist might add that a good tax should be:

● **Efficient** – Taxes distort economic incentives. Low tax rates on income and profits **sharpen incentives** to work and invest in the economy. It is hoped that this strategy will **boost the productive potential** of the economy and shift the AS curve outwards.

● **Harmonised** with the tax systems of other countries. This is especially important in a single market such as the EU.

There are several useful concepts in assessing whether a tax is equitable:

● The **ability to pay principle** says that those with higher incomes should pay more. This may be in absolute terms or as a percentage of income (implying a progressive tax).

● The **benefit principle** suggests that those who receive more services from the government should pay more taxes. This 'you get what you pay for' principle might imply reduced taxes for those who pay for private education or healthcare.

It is especially important in a single market such as the EU, that taxes should be harmonised.

Taxes and equity

Horizontal equity is concerned with the fair treatment of people whose circumstances are the same (e.g. those with the same level of income). For example, the idea that people with a similar ability to pay taxes should pay the same or similar amounts.

Vertical equity relates to the fair treatment of people whose circumstances differ (e.g. those with different incomes). For example, the idea that people with a greater ability to pay taxes should pay more.

Is a high tax burden damaging?

The tax burden is the government's taxation revenue expressed as a percentage of GDP. The tax burden varies over time and from country to country. A high tax burden is seen as a problem for a number of reasons:

● A high tax burden can act as a **disincentive** to economic activity. High corporation taxes may discourage enterprise. This will shift the AS curve to the left in the long run and constrain economic growth. High rates on income tax may provide a disincentive to work and could limit the growth potential of the economy.

● A high tax burden may make the economy **uncompetitive**. For example, by discouraging foreign direct investment or discouraging skilled workers from coming to a country.

● The impact of a high tax burden depends partly on the **composition** of tax revenue. It could be argued that taxing demerit goods tackles a significant market failure and might be desirable.

● The impact of a high tax burden depends partly on how **productively** the tax revenue is used. High quality public services, such as healthcare and education, might be regarded as something worth paying for.

● A high tax burden may be desirable if it is associated with a policy to reduce inequality. Higher income taxes would make the distribution of income more equitable, but might create significant disincentive effects. There is a clear **equity-efficiency trade-off**.

Chapter

20

Unit 4: Measuring the macroeconomy → How the macroeconomy works →
Macroeconomic performance → **Macroeconomic policy tools** → International Economics

Monetary Policy

Monetary policy

Monetary policy can be used to influence the level of AD. It is used primarily to counter inflation, although it can be used to promote economic growth too.

Monetary policy covers the following areas: the interest rate, the money supply and exchange rates.

A contractionary (tight) monetary policy is associated with a:	An expansionary (loose) monetary policy is associated with a:
● High interest rate	● Low interest rate
● Restricted money supply	● Money supply allowed to grow
● Strong exchange rate	● Weak exchange rate

Interest rates

In general, **interest rates** measure the **rate of return on savings** and the **cost of borrowed money**. There is clearly more than one interest rate in the economy. **Secured loans** (such as mortgages – where the house can be repossessed if the borrower fails to meet repayments) carry a lower rate of interest than **unsecured personal loans**, which carry a greater risk to the lender. Credit cards also carry a high rate of interest, as this is the price the borrower pays for 'borrowing on demand'. **Financial intermediaries**, such as banks and building societies, charge higher rates to borrowers than they do to savers. However, the government (or the central bank on its behalf – the Bank of England in the UK) sets the official base rate for the economy and this influences other interest rates.

Money supply

There is no single definition of the money supply. The different definitions are explored later in this chapter.

Exchange rates

The exchange rate is the price of one currency in terms of another, determined by the demand and supply of currencies on the foreign exchange markets.

The functions of money

Money is any asset that is acceptable in the payment of transactions or in the settlement of debts. Money is defined by its functions. These can be summarised as follows:

1. **Medium of exchange** – money allows economic agents to exchange goods without the need for barter.

2. **Store of value** – individuals can choose to forgo consumption in the current time period and save to increase their spending power in the future. They are more likely to do this when money holds its value. Inflation has the effect of reducing the **internal purchasing power of money**.

3. **Unit of account** – this enables us to compare the relative prices of goods and services in pounds and pence.

4. **Standard of deferred payment** – money allows payment for goods and services consumed today in a future time period. For example, this could include the mortgage on a house or a loan to purchase a car.

Besides being able to carry out the four functions, money should have other desirable characteristics. It should be **limited in supply** (otherwise it would have no value), **portable** (notes are preferable to coins in this regard), **durable** (coins preferable to notes) and **divisible** into smaller units (e.g. pounds can be divided into pence).

Liquidity

An asset is liquid if it can be turned into cash easily without any significant financial penalty. Financial assets tend to be more liquid than physical assets.

A spectrum of liquidity:

Most liquid   **Least liquid**

Cash	Current account deposits	Savings account deposits (notice must be given to make withdrawals)	Other financial assets (e.g. stocks and shares)	Cars	Houses

Defining the money supply

There are a number of definitions of the money supply. **Narrow definitions** include only very liquid assets. **Broad definitions** of money contain some less liquid assets.

The UK currently has two main measures of the money supply:

- **M0 (Narrow money)** – consists of Sterling notes and coins in circulation outside the Bank of England, plus the operational balances of commercial banks at the Bank of England. Over 99% of M0 is made up of notes and coins so this form of money is used mainly as a medium of exchange.

- **M4 (Broad money)** – consists of Sterling notes and coins and all Sterling deposits held at UK financial institutions by the private sector. It includes **deposits** held by the private sector (households and firms) for transactions and savings purposes at banks and building societies. It also includes new money created by **lending** in the form of **loans** and **overdrafts**.

Banks are able to create money by lending because only a small percentage of bank deposits needs to be held by the bank in cash. This is because while there is confidence in a bank's financial position it is unlikely that all customers will withdraw their deposits simultaneously. When this does happen it is known as a 'run on the bank' as famously occurred at Northern Rock in 2007.

The UK's monetary policy framework

In recent years, the money supply has been used primarily as an economic indicator rather than as an active instrument of policy. However, in 2009 the Bank of England embarked on a programme of '**quantitative easing**' to boost the money supply with a view to preventing deflation.

The main instrument for UK monetary policy is the official interest rate. The official interest rate is set by the Monetary Policy Committee (MPC) at its monthly meetings. The rate is set independently from the government. This prevents political objectives interfering with the goal of maintaining low and stable inflation; this is a possible source of government failure. The MPC consists of five members from the Bank of England and four independent experts. Interest rates are set to enable the economy to meet the 2% inflation target. The target relates to the CPI measure of inflation. It is a **symmetrical target**, with a 1% boundary either side, so that it is acceptable for inflation to fluctuate between 1% and 3%.

In the event that inflation falls out of its target range, the Governor of the Bank of England must write an open letter of explanation to the Chancellor of the Exchequer. This increases the **accountability** of the Bank of England.

The transmission mechanism

The transmission mechanism refers to the ways in which the official interest rate feeds through the economy to influence inflation. This is illustrated in Figure 20.1.

Figure 20.1: The monetary policy transmission mechanism

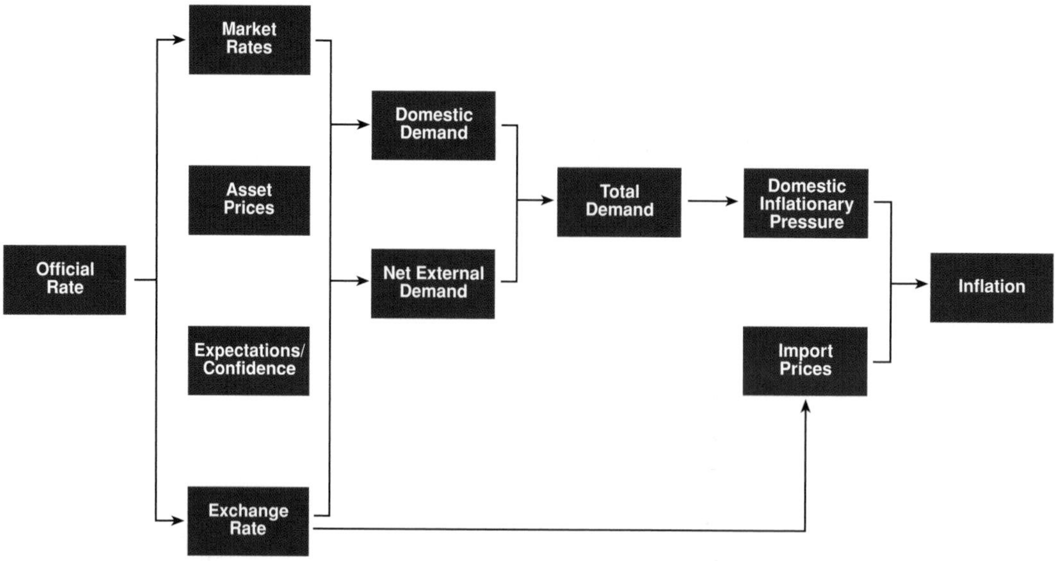

Suppose it was thought necessary to raise interest rates to prevent inflation exceeding its target. This may feed through the economy in the following ways:

Consumption will fall because there will be:

● A **rise in saving**. This is because the opportunity cost of spending has increased.

● A **fall in demand for consumer durables** purchased on credit. This is because loan repayments will increase.

● A fall in '**effective disposable incomes**'. The rise in variable mortgage interest payments will reduce homeowners' ability to spend. Furthermore the demand for housing will fall. If the value of housing and other assets falls, consumers' wealth will diminish and, as a result, they may cut back on their spending.

Investment will fall because a rise in interest rates will increase the cost of investment relative to the yield and, as a result, some investment projects will become unprofitable.

Expectations/confidence. Consumers and firms tend to be less confident when interest rates are rising. This will constrain consumption and investment.

Exchange rate. If a nation's interest rates increase, and are higher than other countries, there is likely to be an inflow of hot money. This is money that can be moved between institutions and countries at short notice in order to take advantage of a higher return on saving. An inflow of hot money will boost demand for the currency and cause an appreciation in the exchange rate. UK goods will be more expensive when priced in a foreign currency and, as a result, demand for UK exports should fall. At the same time, imports become cheaper and, as a result, the demand for imports should rise.

All these transmission mechanisms will reduce aggregate demand and help tackle demand pull inflation. This can be illustrated using diagrams such as Figure A2.6 from Appendix 2.

While the interest rate primarily influences AD, its effect on the **exchange rate** means that it can also affect the costs of production. When Sterling is strong, imported products and raw materials are cheaper. This helps restrict **cost push inflation**.

Evaluating the current policy framework

The following points can be used to evaluate the UK's current policy framework:

- The independence of the MPC from the government is necessary to prevent political interference. This makes it more likely that **low and stable inflation** can be maintained. This should promote investment and enhance the long term performance of the economy.

- Independence and accountability (the need for an open letter if the acceptable range for inflation is breached) may help create policy **credibility**. This should anchor inflationary expectations at the target of 2%. If inflation departs significantly from the target for any length of time, however, **inflationary expectations** are likely to adjust. Significant periods of above target inflation could cause a **wage-price spiral**.

- If the policy credibility is established, the short run unemployment/inflation trade off becomes more favourable. In Figure 18.4(b) a fall in inflationary expectations from 4% to 2% results in a move back to SRPC1 (from SRPC2).

Housing bubbles: asset prices may be fuelled unsustainably by long periods of low inflation and low interest rates.

- Monetary policy works primarily on the demand side of the economy and is therefore not effective in dealing with **supply side shocks**. Supply side shocks are inflationary but also slow economic growth. The requirement to meet the inflation target may mean that the interest rate has to be raised in response to a supply side shock, and this will further damage economic growth.

- A target of low and stable inflation may introduce a **deflationary bias** into policy. However, this is limited by the use of a symmetrical target range.

- The success of policy making depends on an accurate reading of the medium term path of the economy. Changes to the official interest rate take 18-24 months to feed through into the economy. An interest rate set now may be inappropriate by the time it fully impacts on the economy.

- **Empirical data**. The MPC had control of interest rates for a full ten years before the target range of inflation was breached for the first time. This suggests a degree of success although other factors, such as intense global competition, technological advances and productivity improvements, may have played a part. However, in 2008 and 2009 inflation stayed above target for some considerable time, even as a financial crisis and the onset of recession threatened future deflation.

- Some have argued that the policy framework explained in this chapter takes insufficient account of **asset prices**. Long periods of low inflation may permit low interest rates that fuel bubbles in asset markets such as housing. This may sow the seeds of future economic problems. This argument was advanced by some economists to explain the role of the housing market in causing the financial and economic crisis from 2008 onwards.

Chapter

21

Unit 4: Measuring the macroeconomy → How the macroeconomy works →
Macroeconomic performance → **Macroeconomic policy tools** → International Economics

Supply Side Policy

This topic area is covered by the AS level specifications. However, your A2 studies have extended your knowledge of some specific supply side policies. See Chapter 9 on privatisation and deregulation (supply side policies in product markets) and Chapter 18 on unemployment (flexible labour market policies).

It is helpful at this stage to include the following box, which appears at the start of each chapter on macroeconomic policy in the AS Level Revision Guide:

Macroeconomic policy tools are the instruments at the disposal of the government to help it achieve its main economic objectives:

Strong, sustainable economic growth, low unemployment, low and stable inflation and a satisfactory position on the current account of the balance of payments.

The main **demand side** policies are **fiscal** policy and **monetary** policy. The primary role for demand side policies is to stabilise the economy in the short term, smoothing out the business cycle and preventing the problems of slow or negative growth with high unemployment on the one hand, or inflation on the other.

The successful application of demand side policies:

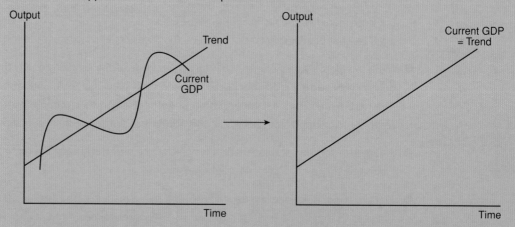

The role of **supply side policy** is to promote the long term health of the economy, boosting the trend growth rate.

The successful application of supply side policies:

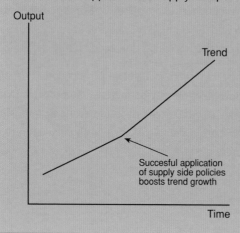

Supply side policies

Supply side policies are policies that aim to:

● **increase productivity**
● **improve incentives** and
● **improve the efficiency of resource allocation** in order to **boost the trend growth rate** (potential growth) of the economy and shift the aggregate supply curve to the right.

A distinctive feature of supply side policies is that they usually involve reducing the role of the government in the economy. Supply side policies are market orientated policies that reflect a belief that the private sector of the economy uses resources more efficiently than the public (government) sector.

It is important to remember that the trend (potential) growth rate of the economy reflects the rate at which the economy's capacity grows and that capacity is a function of the quantity and quality of the four factors of production: land, labour, capital and enterprise.

Figure 21.1 shows the effects of the successful application of supply side policies.

Figure 21.1: Supply side policies

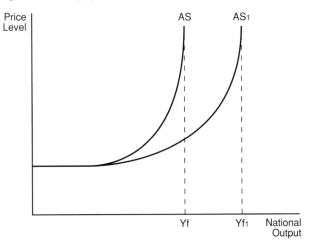

(1) Labour market policies

Supply side policies in the labour market aim to improve the skills of the labour force (**human capital**), promote **labour mobility, remove barriers** that prevent wages reaching equilibrium levels and encourage **flexible working practices** (part-time work, shift work, temporary contracts) that help control costs of production. Specific examples include:

● Income tax cuts to improve incentives to work.

● Cuts in benefit payments to make voluntary unemployment less affordable.

● Tax relief on income earned from renting out accommodation. The rented housing sector promotes labour mobility.

● Removal of the national minimum wage so that the labour market can reach equilibrium.

● Measures to reduce the power of trade unions.

● Reduced government regulation of labour markets to lower the non-wage costs of taking on workers.

● Financial help for firms that invest in the training of workers.

● Changes to the education system to broaden access to further and higher education and to promote vocational training.

(2) Product market policies	Product market policies aim to offer encouragement to private sector firms and to promote competition. Examples include: ● Privatisation, such as the sale of state owned firms to private shareholders. ● Deregulation of markets to open them up to new competition. This occurred in the UK gas and electricity markets, which were at one time statutory monopolies with a single supplier. ● Tax relief on profits retained by firms for investment purposes.
(3) Policies in financial markets	It is important that firms have access to finance in order to invest and innovate. Supply side policies in this area focus on making finance more readily available. One example in the UK was the creation of the Alternative Investment Market (AIM) to allow firms not yet ready to be listed on the Stock Exchange to raise share capital.
(4) Policies to encourage enterprise	Policies to encourage enterprise include: ● Low corporation tax, to increase the profit incentive and stimulate investment. ● Reduced regulation of business. The rules imposed on business by government are sometimes known as 'red tape' and the aim of supply side policies would be to reduce these bureaucratic requirements. Even the length of time to go through the administrative processes of starting up a company can vary widely from country to country. ● Patents to allow those who innovate to exploit the commercial potential of their ideas free from competition for an initial period of time.
Potential benefits of supply side policies	Supply side policies are often thought vital to the long term health of the economy. While **demand side** policies can be used to **stabilise** the economy in the short run, increasing **long run prosperity** depends primarily on the **trend growth rate**. By boosting the **trend growth rate**, supply side policies have the potential to improve simultaneously all the four main macroeconomic objectives. The increased capacity of the economy allows a higher GDP to be generated. This will boost **economic growth**. **Unemployment will fall**, as higher output in the economy will generate an increased demand for labour. Higher capacity and improved efficiency will lower costs and dampen **cost push inflationary pressure**. This helps **improve price competitiveness**, while some of the new capacity can be used to serve the export market. This **improves the current account** of the balance of payments.
Potential costs of supply side policies	Supply side policies are not a solution to all economic ills. They **do not act quickly**; demand side policies are more appropriate for stabilising the economy when a rapid response is needed. Furthermore, in practice, **increases in an economy's trend growth rate are very difficult** to bring about and, after years of supply side measures, UK labour productivity still lags behind other leading nations, such as the USA and Germany. A further problem with supply side policies is that, while they may be **efficient**, it is a matter of opinion as to whether they are **equitable**. For example, flexible working practices benefit some people (such as parents with childcare commitments to juggle) but leave others exposed to insecurity, not knowing how long their employment will last and how many hours they will be asked to work in a week. Supply side measures, such as reductions in trade union power and abolishing minimum wages, also leave workers vulnerable. It is possible that there is an **equity-efficiency trade-off** in the labour market.

Chapter 22

Unit 4: Measuring the macroeconomy → How the macroeconomy works → Macroeconomic performance → Macroeconomic policy tools → **International Economics**

International Trade and Comparative Advantage

Why does trade take place?

Trade can bring benefits to both consumers and firms, which increases the overall level of **economic welfare**.

1. Trade can lead to an improvement in overall economic welfare if countries specialise in the products in which they have a productive advantage. This concept is explained in greater detail below when we examine the law of comparative advantage. Gains from trade occur in the form of **higher output** (economic growth).

2. There are some goods that cannot be produced in the UK because of inappropriate resources and the wrong climate. Good examples include bananas, bauxite and gold. We need to **export** goods to fund **imports** of these items.

3. Trade allows firms to exploit **economies of scale** by operating in much larger markets. Economies of scale lead to lower average costs of production and can be passed onto consumers in the form of lower prices. The UK's membership of the EU gives British firms access to an enormous market. The twenty seven member nations of the EU have over 495 million consumers between them.

4. **International competition** stimulates greater technical efficiency. Lower average costs should feed through to lower prices in the shops and increase **consumer surplus**. Overseas competition can also stop domestic monopolies from exploiting their position.

5. Trade enhances **consumer choice**. When a British consumer purchases a new television there is a tremendous range of products from which to choose. Without trade, consumers would have a relatively limited choice, which could reduce their welfare.

6. Trade leads to a faster rate of **technological diffusion**. This leads to the development of better quality products for consumers and enhances their overall standard of living.

Absolute advantage

A country has an **absolute advantage** in the production of a good or service if it can produce that product using fewer factors of production than another nation (that is, more cheaply).

In the example matrix below, production possibilities are shown if two countries each devote 50% of their resources to manufacturing the products shown.

	DVD Players	**Mobile Phones**
UK	1000	500
Japan	2400	800
Total Output	3400	1300

Japan has an **absolute advantage** over the UK in the production of both DVD players and mobile phones. This is because with an equal amount of resources allocated to both products, Japan can produce more DVD players and mobile phones.

Comparative advantage

Comparative advantage means being able to produce a product at lower opportunity cost than other nations.

In the example above, it is possible quickly to confirm that Japan has a comparative advantage in producing DVD players, where it is more than twice as efficient than the UK. Japan is less than twice as efficient at producing mobile phones. By implication, the UK has a comparative advantage in producing mobile phones.

This can be confirmed by calculating the opportunity cost:

● Suppose the UK wished to increase the production of mobile phones, the opportunity cost of each extra mobile phone is two DVD players (1000/500). For Japan, the same decision has an opportunity cost of three DVD players (2400/800). Therefore, the UK has a comparative advantage in mobile phones because it has to give up fewer DVD players than Japan.

● Suppose Japan wished to increase production of DVD players, the opportunity cost of one extra DVD player is $^1/_3$ of a mobile phone (800/2400). For the UK the same decision has an opportunity cost of $^1/_2$ of a mobile phone (500/1000). Thus, Japan has the comparative advantage in DVD players because it has to give up fewer mobile phones than the UK.

Gains from trade

Gains from trade are increases in total output that occur as a result of specialisation and trade.

According to the theory of **comparative advantage**, there are possible gains from trade if each country specialises in the product where it has a comparative advantage. This remains true even in this example, where Japan has an absolute advantage in both products.

Suppose the UK now specialises completely in producing mobile phones, while Japan allocates 75% of its resources into DVD players and the remaining 25% into mobile phones. The new output levels would be as follows, with a higher output of both products.

Output after specialisation

	DVD Players	Mobile Phones
UK	0	1000
Japan	3600	400
Total Output (gain after specialisation)	3600 (+200)	1400 (+100)

By applying the principle of comparative advantage, total output of DVD players has increased by 200, while production of mobile phones has risen by 100. This represents a gain in **economic welfare**. Although total output has increased, consumers in the UK are unable to purchase DVD players unless trade occurs. If trade takes place, not only will total output rise, but **consumption will also increase**.

Terms of trade

While we have demonstrated that specialisation can increase world output, how this output is divided between nations depends on the prices at which trade takes place, known as the **terms of trade**.

For a nation, the terms of trade can be summarised as:

Terms of trade = (Index of export prices/index of import prices) x 100.

When a nation's terms of trade increase, this is regarded as an **improvement**. This is because the relative price of its exports has risen and it now has to sell fewer units of exports for each unit of imports it buys. Note, however, that such 'improvements' in terms of trade can happen for undesirable reasons, such as a high rate of inflation relative to other countries.

In our example, the UK can produce mobile phones at an opportunity cost of two DVD players. It will not therefore accept less than two DVD players for each mobile phone when it trades. Japan has an opportunity

The UK might decide to specialise in the production of mobile phones.

cost of three DVD players for each mobile produced domestically. It will therefore not pay more than three DVD players for each mobile it buys from the UK. Thus, for mutually beneficial trade, the terms of trade must lie between the domestic opportunity cost ratios.

When the UK split its resources evenly between DVD players and mobile phones there were 1000 DVD players available for consumption. After specialisation, UK consumers would have been unable to purchase DVD players as the country specialised totally in mobile phones. For specialisation and trade to be beneficial, UK consumers will want to be able to consume more DVD players than they did before the country specialised in producing mobile phones. Let us suppose that the UK imports 1050 DVD players from Japan to achieve this goal. If the two countries trade at a rate of exchange of 2.5 DVD players for 1 mobile phone the UK must export 420 mobile phones to Japan (1050/2.5). The post trade situation is illustrated in the table below. The figures in brackets represent the trade flows between the countries.

Post trade allocation

	DVD Players	Mobile Phones
UK	1050 (+1050)	580 (-420)
Japan	2550 (-1050)	820 (+420)
Total Output	3600	1400

Compared with the pre-specialisation output levels, consumers in both countries now have an increased supply of both goods from which to choose. Total output and consumption has increased, and both countries have benefited from specialisation and trade.

Assumptions of comparative advantage theory

It is important to remember that the law of comparative advantage is based on a number of underlying assumptions:

● There are **two countries that produce only two goods** – this assumption is made to keep the explanation as simple as possible, but the model can be applied to the world economy where a wide variety of goods and services are produced.

● **Perfect occupational mobility of factors of production** – this means that resources can be easily transferred from mobile phone to DVD player production.

● **Constant returns to scale** (i.e. doubling the input leads to a doubling of output) – it is assumed that the opportunity cost ratios stay constant as resources are transferred from one industry to another. If businesses exploit increasing returns to scale when they specialise, the potential gains from trade are much greater. However, if decreasing returns to scale set, in the gains from trade may not materialise.

● **Zero transportation costs** – if we introduce transport costs into the model, then any comparative advantage a country may have could well be eliminated. The implementation of **tariffs** will have the same effect.

What factors determine comparative advantage?

If an economy has a comparative advantage in one good, there is no guarantee that it will last forever. Comparative advantages change all the time. Some businesses enjoy a comparative advantage in one product for several years and then lose this advantage when rival producers from other countries enter their markets.

For a country, the following factors are important in determining the relative costs of production and, therefore, comparative advantage:

● The **quantity and quality of factors of production available** – for example, a country with a larger and more skilled workforce is more likely to have a comparative advantage in the production of manufactured goods.

● **Investment in research & development** – may give a nation's firms cost advantages through the development of superior production techniques. R&D may allow firms to develop products and techniques that they can patent. This will give these firms a significant advantage in the market place.

● Movements in the **exchange rate** – a country with a lower cost of production may not be able to exploit this relative cost advantage fully as the prices of goods and services in international markets are distorted by the exchange rate. For example, a rise in value of a currency will increase the price of exports on international markets. This might eliminate any relative cost advantage.

● **Long term rates of inflation** – if a country has a higher inflation rate than other countries it will lose competitiveness on international markets. As a result, it may lose its comparative advantage in certain areas.

● **Import controls**, such as tariffs, can be used to create an artificial comparative advantage for a country's domestic producers (see notes below). By raising the price of imports, a government can protect domestic firms from more efficient foreign producers.

● **Non-price competitiveness** of producers – consumers do not just purchase products because they are cheaper than substitutes. Non-price factors such as product design, reliability, quality and after-sales support are also important in determining comparative advantage.

Chapter

23

Unit 4: Measuring the macroeconomy → How the macroeconomy works →
Macroeconomic performance → Macroeconomic policy tools → **International Economics**

Protectionism

Protectionism

Protectionist policies are designed to shelter domestic firms from overseas competition. There are various methods of protectionism, as outlined below:

● **Tariffs** – a tariff is a tax on imports which can be used to restrict imports and raise revenue for the government.

● **Quotas** – are physical limits that are placed on the level of imports coming into a country. For example, the EU places a limit on the volume of textile imports entering the EU from China.

● **Subsidies** – these are government payments to firms to encourage domestic production. The subsidy lowers the costs of production and makes firms artificially competitive in international markets.

● **Embargoes** – are a total ban on imported goods. These are usually introduced for political or strategic reasons. For example, the USA has an embargo on all Cuban products.

● **Voluntary Export Restraint Agreements** (**VERs**) – these are agreements between counties that limit trade in certain products to a specific quota. For example, Russia has voluntarily agreed to limit its exports of steel to the USA.

● **Administrative Barriers** – countries can make it difficult for firms to import by imposing restrictions and being 'deliberately' bureaucratic. These trade barriers range from stringent safety and specification checks to long hold-ups at customs.

The welfare effects of a tariff

A tariff is a tax levied on the value of imports.

Domestic consumers can purchase goods in an international market from either domestic or foreign suppliers. It is assumed in Figure 23.1 that an infinite number of foreign goods can be purchased at a constant world price P. This means that the world supply curve for the product is perfectly elastic at price P.

Figure 23.1: The welfare effects of a tariff

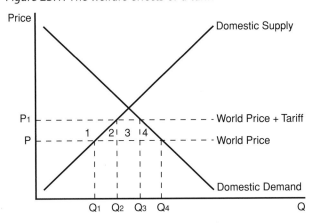

● In the pre-tariff situation at world price P, domestic supply is Q1 and domestic demand is Q4. The difference is met by imports (Q1-Q4). The implementation of the tariff effectively raises the world price to P1. Domestic supply expands to Q2, while demand contracts to Q3. The new post-tariff level of imports is Q2-Q3. If there is no retaliation by other countries this fall in imports may reduce a current account deficit.

● The rise in price reduces the level of consumer surplus by the Area 1 + 2 + 3 + 4. Although consumer welfare has been reduced, domestic producers and the government both gain from the tariff.

- Producer surplus has increased by Area 1. The expansion in domestic output means that producers also receive Area 2 in the form of higher revenue. The expansion in domestic output may also lead to a rise in employment.

- The government receives revenue from the tariff equal to Area 3. This is calculated by multiplying the tariff by the level of imports Q2-Q3.

- Part of the fall in consumer surplus is not redistributed to any economic agent. Area 4 represents the deadweight welfare cost of the tariff.

The effectiveness of a tariff in reducing the level of imports is determined by the elasticity of demand and supply. The more price elastic the demand and supply curves, the greater the fall in imports will be following the implementation of a tariff.

Arguments for protectionism

The law of comparative advantage suggests there are significant gains from trade. In reality, however, free trade creates winners and losers. The losers tend to be those nations with poor international competitiveness who cannot compete in global markets. There are a number of economic arguments that can justify the implementation of import controls, and these are examined below:

(1) Infant industry argument

Some economists believe that it is possible to select certain industries that possess a **potential comparative advantage**. These industries may not yet be able to compete because they have not been able to fully exploit **economies of scale**. Short term protection from established foreign competition will allow the **infant industry** to grow and develop its comparative advantage. Once the industry is competitive, the import control can be removed. The danger is that an infant industry, free of the disciplines of foreign competition, will never achieve full efficiency. It can also be argued that in an ever-changing global marketplace it is very difficult to predict which industries will be successful in the future.

Free trade creates winners and losers – and losers may resort to import controls.

(2) Protection-ism against dumping	**Dumping** refers to the sale of a good below its cost of production. In the short term, consumers benefit from lower priced foreign goods but, in the longer term, persistent undercutting of domestic prices will force domestic producers out of business. With no domestic competition the foreign firm may be able to establish itself as a **monopoly**. Import controls on products sold below their cost of production can, therefore, be justified to prevent the long term exploitation of the consumer, but not if the evidence suggests that the dumping is only of a short term nature offering the consumer a bargain.

(3) Adjusting for externalities

Protectionism can also be used to take account of **negative externalities**, produced by certain goods and services. Goods such as tobacco, firearms and illegal drugs all have adverse social effects. Protectionism can safeguard society from the importation of these goods, by imposing high tariffs or by banning the importation of the good altogether.

It should also be noted that the transportation of goods in international trade carries significant environmental costs. Some argue that trade should be conducted in localised trading blocs of neighbouring countries, rather than globally. This might justify the use of protectionist policies against the products of countries from outside of the trading bloc.

Other reasons for protectionism

Some arguments for protectionism do not work in the best interests of the world economy. Governments tend to place the protection of their nation's interests above the welfare of the world economy. In this sense many of the following policies are driven by a degree of economic nationalism.

- Countries may choose not to **over specialise** in the areas where they possess a comparative advantage. One of the potential dangers of over specialisation is that unemployment may rise quickly if an industry moves into structural decline as new international competition emerges.

- Restriction on imports may improve the **current account balance**.

- The government may also wish to protect against high levels of imports to maintain domestic employment and boost economic growth.

- Protectionism through the use of tariffs will provide the government with a source of revenue.

- Protection may also be used to prevent trade with certain countries on political grounds.

It is also worth remembering that governments are often under political pressure from domestic producers to offer protection. This is a likely source of **government failure** as political and economic objectives come into conflict.

Chapter 24

Unit 4: Measuring the macroeconomy → How the macroeconomy works → Macroeconomic performance → Macroeconomic policy tools → **International Economics**

Globalisation

What is globalisation?

Globalisation describes the process of the world becoming more like a single economy. The economic barriers that divide one economy from another are reduced or removed over time, allowing economies to become more integrated.

Specific elements of globalisation include:

1. **Free movement of goods and services.** This implies that more trade takes place between countries, with a greater proportion of world output traded.

2. **Free movement of labour.** People are increasingly free to move around the world both for leisure and for work purposes. Labour markets for those with high skill levels (e.g. executives) are globalised. For example, UK companies are likely to recruit a chief executive from elsewhere in the EU or from the US.

3. **Free movement of economic capital.** Large companies are now likely to be multinational corporations. Rather than being based in one country, multinationals have production facilities outside their country of origin. The ability to attract Foreign Direct Investment (FDI) is important to the economic prospects of many countries.

4. **Free movement of financial capital.** Financial capital is increasingly mobile and its owners can move capital around the world in search of the highest rate of return. For example, the sub-prime mortgage crisis that began in the USA and triggered the financial crisis that began in 2008 was caused partly by an influx of financial capital from China.

5. **Cultural factors.** There is a greater degree of cultural exchange between countries. For example, brands such as McDonalds and Coca Cola can be found in many countries where cultural values have traditionally been opposed to capitalism.

Measuring globalisation

The headline statistic for measuring the extent of globalisation is the **percentage of world output that is traded**. This percentage has increased significantly in the past few decades. While real world GDP trebled in the three decades to 2000, the volume of exports of goods and services increased more than five fold.

Other statistics are also relevant, including the scale of international capital flows and the international movement of labour.

Why has globalisation occurred?

A number of forces have driven globalisation. These include:

● **Multilateral trade agreements** brokered by international organisations, notably the World Trade Organisation. These agreements have reduced tariff barriers and other protectionist measures that previously restricted trade.

● **Technological advances**, including devices making business communication easier. Video conferencing and e-mail have helped facilitate global business links. The internet has made it easier for consumers in one country to purchase goods directly from foreign firms.

● **Cheaper transportation** of goods and services, especially by air.

● **The collapse of communism** in countries such as the Soviet Union has led to greater economic integration. Former communist countries were largely closed economies. Nowadays, the former Soviet states and countries of Eastern Europe fully participate in the global economy.

- The **increased openness** of some of the world's largest developing economies to trade, notably India and China. Their plentiful labour forces and low wages have made them extremely competitive in international markets and stimulated trade.

- **Outward looking, export orientated development strategies.** Many developing countries have opted for an outward looking development strategy. For example, development is based around the export of low cost manufactured goods.

- **The reduction and removal of controls on the flow of capital** from one country to another.

- **The relaxation of visa regulations** that previously restricted international labour mobility.

The main argument in favour of globalisation is based around the theory of comparative advantage. There are potential gains from trade if each country specialises production where it has a comparative advantage. This can be illustrated using the numerical example shown in Chapter 22.

The economic impact of globalisation (evaluation)

Globalisation should improve the worldwide allocation of resources. If globalisation results in a decline in the use of protectionist policies, the **deadweight welfare loss** that results from trade restrictions might be reduced. The fall in economic welfare caused by protectionism can be illustrated by using the tariff diagram (Figure 23.1) in Chapter 23.

It should be noted that any increased world output that results from specialisation might not be evenly distributed. Some countries may not necessarily be better off. This depends on the price at which trade takes place (the terms of trade). If the **terms of trade** are beneficial for a country, its consumption possibilities are greater than its production possibilities. However, this is not always the case.

The activities of multinational corporations, especially in developing countries are controversial. Some people regard the employment of low wage labour as exploitation and believe that the lack of regulation in some developing countries is exploited by multinationals to produce low cost output. However, it can be argued that living standards in developing countries would be lower without the investment in capital and training provided by multinationals. Indeed without multinationals, some of those workers employed in low wage industries might be unemployed.

The free movement of goods and services is at the heart of globalisation, but the **international transportation of goods creates substantial environmental externalities**. It could be argued that much of the trade that currently takes place would not be commercially viable if producers were forced to pay a sum towards the environmental damage caused by the worldwide transportation of goods. Instead, the environment is used as if it were a free resource.

Globalisation has made a country's competitiveness in the international economy a much more important determinant of its economic success (see Chapter 25). If a country is not competitive, both in terms of price and non price factors, its rate of economic growth is likely to be curtailed.

Globalisation has imposed adjustment costs. It can be argued that globalisation has imposed costs on developing countries such as the need to adapt to new values and new way of life. Free market capitalism is alien to many traditional cultures. At the same time, globalisation has imposed adjustment costs on many developed nations who have lost comparative advantage in manufacturing to newly industrialised countries and now face challenges in the tertiary (service) and the quaternary (technology and information services) sectors. Globalisation is a source of structural unemployment in developed countries.

Chapter

25

Unit 4: Measuring the macroeconomy → How the macroeconomy works →
Macroeconomic performance → Macroeconomic policy tools → **International Economics**

International Competitiveness

What is international competitiveness?

International competitiveness can be defined as the ability of a nation to compete successfully overseas and sustain improvements in real output and living standards. The concept could also be applied to particular regions within a country.

There are two main factors that determine international competitiveness in markets for goods and services. They are:

● The **price competitiveness** of a country. How do prices compare to those of substitute products made in other countries?

● The **non price competitiveness** of a country. How do factors such as quality, after-sales service and rates of innovation compare to those of substitute products made in other countries?

A firm that is unable to compete effectively on price terms (e.g. due to relatively high wage costs in comparison to competitor nations) may succeed by differentiating its products or by targeting niche markets. This makes demand for the firm's products less elastic, allowing the firm to charge a price premium.

A diagram to illustrate the effects of non price competitiveness is shown in Figure 25.1. Suppose that a firm's production costs mean that it cannot match the cheapest world price for a good, shown as P_1. Instead, the firm charges P_2, but because it is competitive on non price factors, demand for its product is relatively inelastic (D_I) and, as a result, only contracts to Q_2. Had demand been more elastic (D_E) demand would have contracted much more, to Q_3.

Figure 25.1: Non price competitiveness

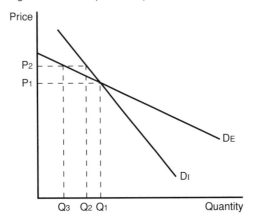

It is also important for a country to be able to compete in markets for factors of production. Factors influencing international competitiveness in this area include:

● **The ability of the country to attract foreign direct investment** from multinational companies. Such investment increases productive capacity and can help to produce long term growth and raise living standards.

● **The ability of the country to produce entrepreneurs** or to attract them from other countries.

● **The ability of the country to attract labour from other nations**, especially highly skilled labour to fill any skills gap that exists. Skills gaps, in areas such as IT and biotechnology, can drive up wages and increase the production costs for firms.

Why has international competitiveness become more important?

International competitiveness has become more important because of the increasingly globalised nature of economies (see Chapter 24). Economies are now more interconnected and **open** to trade than ever before. This makes competitiveness in markets for goods and services more important to each country's standard of living.

Globalisation has also increased the importance of competitiveness in the markets for factors of production. For example, companies are increasingly free to locate wherever they choose around the world. As a result, countries must compete to attract the physical capital provided by **foreign direct investment**, along with the jobs that such investment generates. Technology also plays an important role in determining where a firm locates. For example, developments in telecommunications have allowed UK firms to locate call centres anywhere in the world. Unless UK workers are competitive on wage rates there is a risk that jobs will be lost.

Highly competitive nations are likely to experience stronger trend growth. A competitive nation has a well functioning supply side to its economy. This can be illustrated with appropriate diagrams such as Figure A2.7 or A2.10 from Appendix 2 or Figure 17.1.

Determinants of a nation's competitiveness

There are a number of key determinants of a nation's competitiveness. Some of the most important ones refer to the country's labour markets:

● **Unit labour costs** (**ULCs**). These are the labour costs per unit of output (total labour cost/total output). Unit labour costs rise when wages increase faster than productivity (output per worker). Many newly industrialised countries such as China are highly competitive in manufacturing because their large populations serve to drive down wages and therefore ULCs.

● **The quantity and quality of skills possessed by a nation's workers.** Skill levels influence productivity and the attractiveness of a nation as a location for business.

● **Labour flexibility.** Flexible working practices such as part time work, shift work and temporary contracts help to limit production costs for firms.

Other determinants of competitiveness include:

● **Economic stability.** Businesses are more likely to locate in countries with a reputation for economic stability. For example, firms may be attracted to a country with a track record of low and stable inflation. This aids business planning.

● **Tax regimes.** Favourable tax policies can help boost competitiveness in markets for factors of production. For example, low income tax (especially at high income levels) improves incentives to work and may attract skilled labour. The UK's top rate of tax will rise to 50% in 2010 and there are fears this may cause a '**brain drain**' of talented workers to other countries. Plans to introduce a '**non-dom tax**' on workers earning money in the UK but living (domiciled) in other countries have raised similar fears. Low corporation tax helps make a country an attractive location for business. Governments sometimes offer 'tax sweeteners' (special tax rates or tax relief) to attract **foreign direct investment**. It should be noted, however, that such measures might contravene international agreements on fair competition.

● **Degree of regulation.** Complying with government regulation imposes costs on business and may discourage enterprise. Countries with only 'light touch' regulation tend to be more competitive than those who impose strict regulations on business.

● **Rates of innovation.** This might depend on the proportion of a nation's GDP invested in new capital. However, government policy on education and training and whether sufficient incentives are provided to innovate are also important.

The UK is seen as a gateway to Europe.

Which nations are the most competitive?

In the World Economic Forum's Global Competitiveness Report 2009-2010, the USA was ranked as the world's most competitive nation. The UK was ranked in 11th place, with China in 17th. European countries, including Denmark, Sweden, Finland, Germany and the Netherlands, dominated the top ten. The highest ranking Asian economy (and the only one present in the top ten) was Singapore, in 5th place.

The UK's ability to attract foreign direct investment

The UK has been very successful at attracting foreign direct investment in recent years. Reasons for this include:

● A **skilled labour** force.

● **Flexible labour markets** compared to those of European competitors such as France and Germany.

● These two points have combined to give **lower unit labour costs**.

● The UK is seen as a **gateway to Europe**. The UK's membership of the EU and its single market (see Chapter 28 on trading blocs) means that output produced in the UK can be exported to other EU nations free of tariffs and other protectionist barriers.

● The UK has relatively low tax rates (both the top rate of income tax and corporation tax are set at competitive levels).

● The UK has enjoyed a reputation for stability in its economy and financial system. However, this reputation may be damaged by the effects of the financial and economic crisis that began in 2008.

Chapter

26

Unit 4: Measuring the macroeconomy → How the macroeconomy works →
Macroeconomic performance → Macroeconomic policy tools → **International Economics**

The EU and Trading Blocs

Trading blocs

A trading bloc is a group of countries that have joined together to reduce or eliminate trading barriers between the participating states.

Levels of integration

Integration between participating economies is deeper in some trading blocs than others, as indicated in the following table, which also gives brief details of the development of the European Union.

Direction of increasing integration →

Preference area	Free trade area	Customs union	Single market	Economic/monetary union
Members offer preferential treatment (e.g. lower tariffs) to each other but retain independent tariff policies in relation to non member states.	All tariffs and trade barriers between members are removed but members retain independent tariff policies in relation to non member states.	A free trade area, in addition to which members form a common trade policy in relation to non member states.	Free movement for factors of production, such as labour and capital, is added to the free movement of goods.	Members adopt a single currency, with the implication that there is a single official interest rate across the currency area.
ACP: African Caribbean and Pacific Group (46 countries)	NAFTA: North American Free Trade Agreement (USA, Canada, Mexico)	Mercosur (Argentina, Brazil, Paraguay, Mexico, Venezuela)	EEA: European Economic Area (27 members of the EU plus Iceland, Norway and Liechtenstein)	The Eurozone
		The EU became a Customs Union in 1957 (The Treaty of Rome). It was known as the European Economic Community. The 6 original members (Belgium, France, Germany, Italy, Luxembourg and the Netherlands) had earlier formed the European Coal and Steel Community in 1951.	The Single European Act of 1988 paved the way for the EU to become a single market by 1992.	The Euro was introduced in 11 countries on 1st January 1999 and is now the official currency of 16 countries. The Maastricht Treaty of 1992 set the foundations for the Euro.

Patterns of trade

The pattern of trade describes the amount of trade undertaken by a country, and its composition in terms of which products are traded and with which countries.

Membership of a trading bloc tends to alter a country's pattern of trade in two main ways:

Trade creation

Trade creation involves a shift in spending from a higher cost domestic source to a lower cost source within a trading bloc, as a result of the abolition of tariffs. For example, when the Czech Republic recently joined the EU, Czech consumers may have switched spending on car insurance away from a higher priced Czech supplier towards a German insurance company that had decided to operate in the Czech market. In principle, trade creation stimulates an **increase in trade** and ought to lead to a **more efficient allocation of resources** as each country exploits their comparative advantage.

Trade diversion

Membership of a trading bloc makes trading with other member states more attractive compared to trading with non members. The UK's membership of the EU biases our trade towards other EU member states. This may involve buying products from within the EU that could have been produced more cheaply elsewhere in the world. Non EU products have been made uncompetitive by the tariff charged when the product enters the EU. This can lead to a **misallocation of resources**.

Advantages of trading blocs

The advantages of a trading bloc are:

- Trade creation.

- A larger market may intensify competition and stimulate greater technical efficiency. Lower average costs should feed through to lower prices in the shops.

- Access to a large market may allow firms to generate substantial economies of scale. This will lead to lower average costs of production that can be passed onto consumers in the form of lower prices.

- Access to a larger market may create a greater incentive to invest and encourage a faster rate of technological diffusion. This will increase economic growth and enhance consumer choice.

Disadvantages of trading blocs

The disadvantages of a trading bloc are:

- Trade diversion.

- A larger market, with potential gains from economies of scale will encourage merger activity. Mergers may result in an increase in monopoly power and higher prices for consumers. There will be a need for a competition policy that covers the entire trading bloc and this will impose a large regulatory cost on member countries.

- There is a greater potential for **informational failures** in the larger market created by a trading bloc. Consumers may find it difficult to compare prices across a large number of countries. This problem will be reduced by the creation of a single currency, as this will give greater price transparency.

EU institutions

There are three key policy making bodies within the EU. Some of their decisions affect economic policy.

European Commission	Council of Ministers	European Council
Puts forward new policy proposals and carries out existing policy. Commissioners are nominated by their own national governments but are meant to act independently of them and administer EU policy in the overall interests of the EU.	Examines the policy proposals of the European Commission. Membership changes according to the topic being discussed. If the topic is agriculture, it will be discussed by the agriculture ministers from each EU member state.	This is a summit conference, a meeting of the heads of government of the member states of the EU. Its task is to reach decisions on fundamental aspects of EU policy.

It is helpful to know that policy making bodies are theoretically answerable to the **European Parliament,** members of which are elected by the citizens of member states. However, in practice this role of the European Parliament has been somewhat limited. The European Parliament also passes laws (legally EU law takes precedence over that of member states). The **European Court of Justice** interprets European treaties and laws.

Key EU policy areas

Areas of economic policy in which the EU plays an important role include:

- **Agriculture.** The EU's Common Agricultural Policy (CAP) once accounted for as much as 70% of the EU budget. In theory, it was a buffer stock system. However, it tended to work as a minimum price scheme, as the intervention price was set well above the long run equilibrium. The maintenance of the minimum price required intervention buying and led to the growth of the infamous butter and grain mountains. In recent years, the scheme has been reformed in an attempt to reduce overproduction and waste. The emphasis has shifted from supporting production to paying farmers for being custodians of the countryside.

- **Competition policy.** EU Competition Policy is based on the prohibition of formal collusive agreements and the abuse of dominant positions in markets. It applies in cases involving firms located in more than one member state. Recent modernisation of UK Competition Policy has brought UK policy in line with the EU framework (see Chapter 10).

- **Environmental policy.** Environmental policy (tackling resource degradation and depletion) requires a coordinated approach because the ability of one nation to tackle environmental issues alone is limited. The EU sets environmental standards for air and water quality (regulation) and operates a carbon emissions trading scheme (tradable pollution permits).

- **Fisheries policy.** The EU is keen to tackle the problem of overfishing, which is depleting fish stocks. The current approach is based on quotas (regulation) that restrict catches. This is controversial as it has led to fish that have already been caught being thrown back into the water if they are over a fisherman's quota. Political pressure has also prevented quotas being set at the levels recommended by scientists, and the cost of enforcing the policy has been high. Some economists have also argued that there may be more effective ways of protecting fish stocks.

- **Regional policy.** A significant portion of the EU budget is allocated to policies that encourage economic development in its poorest regions. Examples of projects financed in this way include: getting sites ready for industrial development; building and refurbishing factories; improving transport access to industrial, commercial and tourist developments; training and developing local people; supporting innovation and development; promoting the cultural arts and leisure industries; support measures for small and medium sized companies and work to improve the environment. Note that these measures tend to be focused on improving the supply side performance of impoverished areas.

EU enlargement

The EU has grown since its inception in 1951. This growth has been particularly rapid in the last decade. In 2004, 10 new members from Eastern and Central Europe joined the EU. This enlargement has increased the potential for economies of scale and free trade across a larger area. It offers advantages to consumers in the form of intensified price competition. Firms may be able to benefit from lower production costs if they can take advantage of the lower wages in Eastern and Central Europe. However enlargement does pose significant challenges too. There have been doubts raised about the ability of established members of the EU to cope with large influxes of people from Eastern Europe. There are also concerns about the large disparities in income and wealth created by different levels of development in member states. This will require active support from the governments and, by implication the tax payers, of existing members to help foster economic development in the new member states.

Figure 26.1: EU enlargement

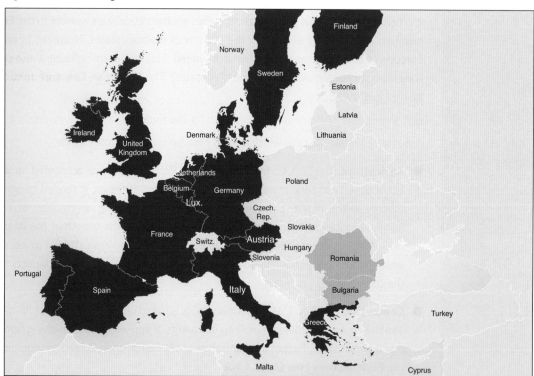

1951	Belgium, Germany, France, Italy, Luxembourg, Netherlands
1973	Denmark, Ireland and UK join
1981	Greece joins
1986	Spain and Portugal join
1995	Austria, Finland and Sweden join (we now have the EU15, shown in blue above)
2004	10 Central and Eastern European Countries join (to form the EU25)
2007	Bulgaria and Romania join (EU27). Turkey is currently seeking membership.

The Euro and Monetary Unions

A monetary union is the ultimate fixed exchange rate system. For example, if the UK were to join the Euro there would be no scope at all for exchange rate fluctuations between the UK and the other 'Eurozone' nations. To understand the economics of a single currency, it is necessary to have a good understanding of fixed exchange rate systems. The impact of the Euro is examined at the end of Chapter 27 on exchange rates.

Chapter 27

Unit 4: Measuring the macroeconomy → How the macroeconomy works →
Macroeconomic performance → Macroeconomic policy tools → **International Economics**

Exchange Rates

Exchange rates

The exchange rate is the price of one currency in terms of another. It is determined by the demand and supply of currencies on the foreign exchange markets (FOREX).

The **effective exchange rate**, or Sterling Index, is a weighted index of Sterling's value against a basket of international currencies. The proportion of trade between the UK and each country determines the size of the weights.

There are different types of exchange rate system:

Floating exchange rates are determined solely by market demand for and supply of the currency. There is no government intervention involved. The exchange rate changes on a minute by minute basis, and the rate at any moment in time is referred to as the **spot exchange rate**. This is different to the **forward exchange rate**, which involves the delivery of currency at some time in the future at an agreed rate. This is often used by companies wanting to reduce the risk of exchange rate uncertainty.

Managed exchange rates involve some government intervention to influence the exchange rate, but the exchange rate is still primarily determined by the forces of demand and supply in FOREX markets. The central bank may use interest rates to influence the demand and supply of the currency, or may use its foreign currency reserves to buy or sell the currency.

Fixed exchange rates are based around a target rate, but the currency can move between permitted bands of fluctuation either side of the target. The authorities attempt to maintain the target rate by adjusting interest rates or using foreign currency reserves. The UK was last in a fixed exchange rate system when it was a member of the European Exchange Rate Mechanism (ERM) in 1992. For example, Sterling was given a target rate against the Deutchmark ($£1 = DM2.95$) but the currency could move 6% either side of the target rate. Most fixed exchange rate systems should properly be called semi-fixed because, like the ERM, the exchange rate is allowed to move within a specified band, perhaps either side of a central target rate.

Supply and demand of currencies

The demand and supply of currencies are determined by the following factors:

Demand for a currency	Supply of a currency
• exports of goods	• imports of goods
• exports of services	• imports of services
• inflows of direct investment	• outflows of direct investment
• inflows of portfolio investment and speculative demand for the currency	• outflows of portfolio investment and speculative selling of the currency
• official buying of the currency by the Central Bank	• official selling of the currency by the Central Bank

In Figure 27.1, the equilibrium exchange rate for the pound and the US dollar is at price P, where supply and demand for Sterling are equal.

If there is an **increase in demand** for the pound, due to a surge in exports to the USA, there will be **upward pressure** on the value of the exchange rate. In Figure 27.2, the demand for Sterling will shift to the right from D to D_1 and the value of the pound will appreciate from P to P_1. Conversely, if there is a fall in demand for Sterling, perhaps due to a fall in foreign direct investment from the USA, the demand for Sterling will shift from D to D_2 and the currency will depreciate from P to P_2.

An **increased supply of pounds**, due to a rise in imports from the USA, will apply **downward pressure** on the value of the currency. In Figure 27.3, the supply of Sterling will shift to the right from S to S_1 and the value of the pound will depreciate from P to P_1. Conversely, if there is a fall in supply for Sterling, perhaps due to a fall in speculative selling of the currency, the supply of Sterling will shift from S to S_2 and the currency will appreciate from P to P_2.

Figure 27.1

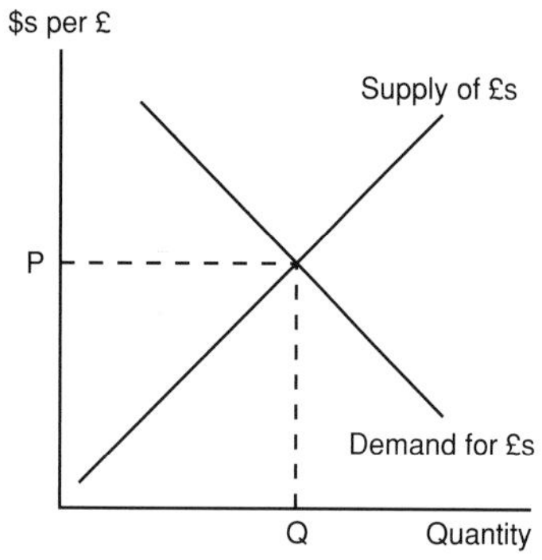

$s per £

Supply of £s

P

Demand for £s

Q   Quantity

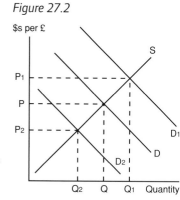

Figure 27.2

$s per £

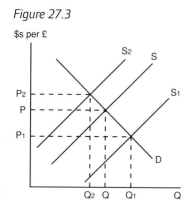

Figure 27.3

$s per £

The value of a country's exchange rate is determined by a number of different factors:

Interest rates and hot money

If a nation's interest rates increase, and are higher than other countries, there is likely to be an inflow of **hot money**. This is money that can be moved between institutions and countries at short notice in order to take advantage of a higher return on saving. An inflow of hot money will boost demand for the currency and cause an appreciation in the exchange rate.

Trade

Selling exports overseas represents a demand for the domestic currency from foreign importers. Similarly when consumers buy imports, they supply their own currency and this is eventually translated into a demand for foreign currencies. When an economy is running a current account deficit (see Chapter 28), supply of the currency exceeds its demand on FOREX markets and this will place downward pressure on the exchange rate.

Inflation and purchasing power parity

The theory of **purchasing power parity** (PPP) explains how changes in domestic prices influence the exchange rate. The theory states that the exchange rate between two countries is in equilibrium when the price of an identical basket of goods and services is the same in both nations.

For example, suppose a basket of goods in the USA is $200 while the price of the same basket in the UK is £100. If £1 = $2, then the exchange rate is in equilibrium, because the price of the basket is the same in both countries. If the price of the basket in the UK now rises to £150, consumers will choose to buy in America instead. This increases the supply of Sterling and demand for the Dollar, causing Sterling to depreciate until purchasing power parity is restored.

If the only reason that people swapped between currencies was for trade, then the exchange rate should be at or close to purchasing power parity. However, exchange rates are influenced by other factors such as flows of hot money and speculation on the future value of the currency.

Economic growth

Countries that suffer a prolonged **recession** often find that their exchange rate weakens. The FOREX markets may see slow growth as a sign of economic weakness and mark down the value of the currency.

When economic growth is above trend, there is danger that demand pull inflation will emerge. This may cause the currency to appreciate as currency traders anticipate that interest rates may rise relative to other countries. Rapid growth may also lead to the 'sucking in' of imports by domestic consumers, implying an increased supply of the currency. This increased supply might cause the currency to depreciate in the long run.

Fiscal policy

The FOREX markets consider a government's fiscal policy (in particular how much it is borrowing) to be a key economic indicator. Countries with strong public sector finances tend to have a stronger exchange rate as a consequence.

Speculation

Currency can be held as an asset by speculators who hope to make a capital gain by buying currencies that are likely to appreciate. It is important not to dismiss the effects that special factors (such as political events, changing commodity prices, etc.) can have on the value of a currency.

Maintaining a fixed exchange rate

When a country operates a fixed exchange rate, the government loses control over other aspects of monetary policy. In particular, maintaining the exchange rate is likely to require that interest rates are kept broadly in line with those of other countries in the fixed exchange rate system. This will prevent flows of hot money from putting upward or downward pressure on the exchange rate.

The need to keep interest rates broadly in line with other countries in the fixed exchange rate system makes it crucial that **convergence** of macroeconomic conditions is achieved between the countries before a country joins a fixed exchange rate system. If convergence does not occur, then the interest rate will not be appropriate to the underlying economic conditions in the country.

Central banks must be willing to use official intervention to preserve the target rate. For example, if the exchange rate is falling too rapidly then the central bank will have to sell foreign exchange reserves to increase demand for the currency

Figure 27.4: Maintaining a fixed exchange rate above market equilibrium

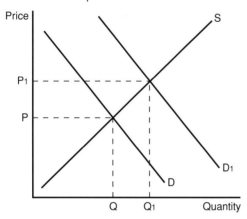

In Figure 27.4, the equilibrium exchange rate P is below the exchange rate target of P1. To move the exchange rate back to the target rate, the authorities can shift demand for the currency to D1 by raising interest rates or buying their own currency using foreign exchange reserves.

Advantages and disadvantages of a fixed exchange rate system

Advantages	Disadvantages
• A fixed rate can reduce uncertainty for exporters and importers, leading to **trade creation**.	• A fixed rate may make trade with other members of the system artificially cheap relative to that with other trade partners, leading to **trade diversion**.
• Greater certainty may help encourage more investment, leading to economic growth.	• Maintaining a fixed rate implies loss of control over interest rates.
• A high fixed exchange rate can help to limit demand pull inflation, as exports become less price competitive in foreign markets. Cost push inflationary pressures will also decline as imports, including those of raw materials, become cheaper.	• If the economy is in recession, the exchange rate cannot fall to restore international competitiveness.
	• History suggests that a fixed exchange rate is difficult to maintain (previous fixed rate systems, such as the ERM, experienced difficulties).
• A low fixed exchange rate can help boost price competitiveness and will raise aggregate demand.	• Speculators may attack a fixed exchange rate if they consider it unrealistic. Sterling was forced out of the ERM in 1992 when it became clear that Sterling's fixed rate was too high and that the UK could not tolerate the high interest rate needed to maintain the target rate.

Economic effects of exchange rate movements	A depreciation in the value of Sterling will have wide ranging economic effects, impacting on the four main macroeconomic indicators.

Exports	<ul><li>Exporters should benefit from a fall in the value of the pound. UK goods will be cheaper when priced in a foreign currency and, as a result, demand for UK **exports should rise**.</li><li>The effect on the demand for exports is determined by the foreign price elasticity of demand for UK goods.</li><li>Exporting firms may decide to hold export prices constant and increase their profit margins.</li></ul>
Imports	<ul><li>A depreciation in Sterling will make imports more expensive and, as a result, the demand for **imports should fall**.</li></ul>
Balance of Payments	<ul><li>Normally a depreciation will **improve the current account balance**. The demand for imports will fall and the demand for exports will rise. However in the short term, if the Marshall-Lerner condition is not satisfied there may be a **'J curve' effect** and the current account will deteriorate (see Chapter 28).</li></ul>
Inflation	<ul><li>A fall in the exchange rate increases import prices in the UK.</li><li>Higher prices for imported components and raw materials may lead to **cost push inflation** (see Chapter 18). The extent to which firms raise their prices depends on the price elasticity of demand for the product.</li><li>Higher exports and lower imports increase aggregate demand and cause **demand pull inflation**.</li></ul>
Economic Growth and Employment	<ul><li>Higher exports and falling imports will **increase aggregate demand and GDP**.</li><li>A rise in aggregate demand should reduce **demand deficient unemployment**.</li></ul>

An appreciation of the exchange rate is likely to have the opposite effect to those described above. Remember that changes in the exchange rate will have a lagged effect on the economy and will not happen instantaneously.

The Euro and Monetary Union	The Euro was launched on 1st January 1999 and is now the official currency of 16 member states of the European Union.
Advantages of the Euro	

- **Trade creation.** More trade takes place for two main reasons. There are no longer any **transaction costs** because it is not necessary to switch between currencies when trading. There is also **reduced risk** because there is no danger of the profit margin in a trade contract being eliminated by unfavourable exchange rate movements.

- **The Euro helps the EU single market function more efficiently.** Nations are better able to exploit their comparative advantage within the EU. The more complete access to the EU's huge market created by Euro membership may help firms better to exploit economies of scale and this encourages investment and economic growth.

- The Euro improves consumer information by creating greater **price transparency**, allowing easier price comparisons.

- Price transparency increases the competitiveness of markets and this reduces the ability of firms to raise prices, **helping hold down inflationary pressures**.

● **Euro membership acts as a discipline on governments.** The loss of sovereignty over monetary policy and exchange rates, and to some extent over fiscal policy too (see the disadvantages section below), means that there is no quick fix solution to economic difficulties. It is, therefore, important that governments pursue policies designed to create stability. As a result, governments have focused on supply side policies to enhance economic performance.

Disadvantages of the Euro

● **Trade diversion.** As trade with firms in other Eurozone nations becomes more attractive, trade may be diverted away from trade with firms in other nations where production costs are lower. A misallocation of resources may result.

● **Loss of control over monetary policy.** A single currency implies a single interest rate (this is sometimes dubbed a 'one-size-fits-all' monetary policy). This limits the ability of national governments to respond to economic shocks (see Chapter 17). The Euro interest rate is set by the European Central Bank (ECB). There are some concerns that ECB's target rate of inflation of less than 2% introduces an excessive anti-inflationary bias to economic policy. As a result, higher interest rates have limited the growth of aggregate demand and caused sluggish economic growth.

● **Fiscal policy constraints.** Budget deficits are limited for Eurozone member states, again restricting the ability of national governments to respond to shocks. The Maastricht Treaty set the limit for budget deficits at 3% of GDP. The purpose of this limit was to prevent excessive spending by member governments threatening the low inflation credibility of the new currency. This limit on the size of budget deficits has been put under severe pressure by the financial and economic crisis that began in 2008.

● **Lack of competitiveness cannot be offset by exchange rate depreciation.** Economies struggling to compete on price usually experience an exchange rate depreciation, helping restore their price competitiveness (see the notes on purchasing power parity earlier in this chapter). This is not possible within a single currency.

● **Problems if convergence is not achieved.** To tolerate a single interest rate, it is vital that the member states of a currency union are converged with one another and are at the same stage of the economic cycle. This was a lesson learnt by the UK when it joined the ERM in 1992. The UK economy was in recession and could not tolerate the same high interest rate needed by the booming German economy. This had a crippling impact on UK economic growth and prolonged the length of the recession.

● **The danger of asymmetric shocks.** Once achieved, convergence between economies is not guaranteed to last. An asymmetric shock is one that affects different economies in different ways. For example, the UK may be more sensitive to interest rate changes than the current members of the Eurozone, because of the high proportion of the UK housing stock that is owner occupied.

● **The Eurozone is not an optimal currency area.** This refers to an area that maximises the efficiency of using a single currency. One of the main criteria for an optimal currency area is that labour is mobile within the area. This does not seem to be the case within the EU given barriers to labour mobility such as those created by different languages and cultures.

Chapter

28

Unit 4: Measuring the macroeconomy → How the macroeconomy works →
Macroeconomic performance → Macroeconomic policy tools → **International Economics**

The Balance of Payments

The Balance of Payments

The UK Balance of Payments accounts are a record of financial transactions between economic agents in the UK and the international economy over a given period of time. Inflows of currency are recorded as a credit and outflows of currency are recorded as a debit.

The current account and capital accounts

The Balance of Payments account is normally split into two sections.

The **current account** records international income and expenditure flows, primarily relating to trade in tangible goods (**visible section** of the current account) and intangible services (the **invisible section**). The invisible section also includes interest, profit and dividends from UK assets owned overseas, matched against outflows of the same from foreign owned assets in the UK. It also includes transfers such as gifts and overseas aid payments.

The **capital account** shows how the current account deficit is financed or how the surplus is used. It records international flows of financial capital, such as cross-border loans and investments in the stocks and shares of other nations. Entries in the capital account can be distinguished from those in the current account by the fact that they create an asset or liability that will necessitate entries in the current account at a future date. For example, consider a cross-border loan. This creates an asset for the lender, because interest must be paid on the loan at a later date. When the interest is received, this constitutes income and is entered in the current account.

The structure of the balance of payments accounts is summarised in Figure 28.1

Figure 28.1

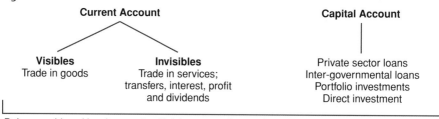

Balance achieved by changes to official reserves; in practice, a balancing item is usually needed

The Balance of Payments accounts sum to zero

The Balance of Payments accounts must sum to zero, because the short fall of foreign currency implied by a **current account deficit** must be obtained by inflows on the capital account, or by running down the nation's foreign currency reserves, which would be shown as a '+' in the accounts. This is analogous to the individual who must borrow, or run down savings, in the event that their expenditure exceeds their income in any given time period.

Equally, for a nation running a **current account surplus**, its capital account shows how this surplus has been used. China has been running a large surplus in recent years and this has allowed it to buy assets around the world (creating debits on its capital account) and accumulate huge currency reserves (largely US Dollars).

Because errors and omissions usually prevent the accounts from balancing, as they should do in theory, a **balancing item** is usually included to make sure the accounts sum to zero.

An overvalued exchange rate may lead to a current account deficit.

Causes of a current account deficit

By definition, if some economies are running current account deficits, then others must be running surpluses. It is important to identify the underlying causes of a current account deficit before designing policies to correct the problem. Some of the more common causes of a current account deficit are:

● **High level of economic growth** – In a boom, when consumption and investment expenditure tend to rise, it is inevitable that some of this increased spending will leave the country through import purchases. This will cause the current account balance to deteriorate. The higher the marginal propensity to import, the greater the increase in imports will be.

● **Lack of productive capacity of domestic firms** – If home producers have insufficient capacity to meet rising demand from consumers then imports of goods and services will be 'sucked in' to satisfy this excess demand. As a result, the current account will worsen.

● **Poor price and non-price competitiveness** (see Chapter 25).

● **Declining comparative advantage in many areas** – The advantages that countries have in producing certain goods and services can change over time, as technology alters and other countries exploit their economic resources and develop competing industries. The UK manufacturing sector, for example, has suffered over the last 30 years from the emergence of low cost production in newly industrialised countries.

● **An over valued exchange rate** – Some economists believe that current account deficits stem from the exchange rate being at too high a level. A high exchange rate causes export prices to be higher in foreign markets whilst imports become relatively cheaper. Other things being equal, this will cause imports to rise, exports to fall and the current account balance to worsen.

● **Falling surplus in an important mineral resource** – some countries rely heavily on the export of specific primary commodities whose prices on international markets might be highly volatile. A fall in price when demand from purchasers is inelastic can cause a sharp fall in total export revenues and a sudden deterioration in a country's current account.

Are current account deficits always a bad thing? (evaluation)

In the short term, a current account deficit can allow a nation's consumers to enjoy a higher standard of living. A **cyclical deficit** may occur during the recovery or boom stage of the business cycle as high levels of demand suck in imports. This is not a major cause for concern if balanced against current account surpluses at other stages of the economic cycle.

However, deficits imply that the country is consuming at a point beyond its production possibility frontier (PPF) as shown in Figure 28.2. The resulting **liabilities** acquired on the capital account imply that consumption must be constrained to meet interest and capital repayments at a later date.

Figure 28.2: A balance of payments deficit

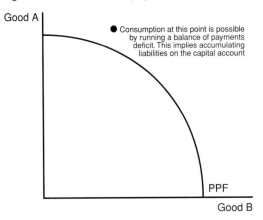

A long term, **structural deficit** in particular may show that the country is 'living beyond its means'. It may be a symptom of a weakening domestic economy and a lack of international competitiveness. For example, it could be a sign of low levels of productivity and high domestic production costs. If imports continue to rise, this will threaten domestic employment and incomes and living standards may fall.

For this reason, governments prefer to avoid substantial and persistent current account deficits (structural deficits). The difference between a cyclical deficit and the more worrying structural deficit is illustrated in Figure 28.3.

Figure 28.3: Cyclical and structural deficits

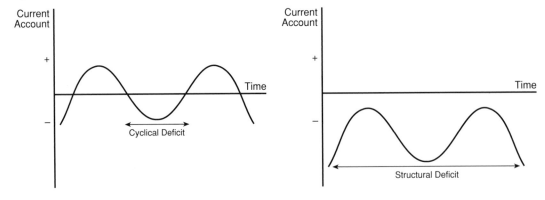

Policies to solve a current account deficit: (1) Expenditure reducing

Expenditure reducing policies aim to reduce the spending of consumers and firms so that demand for imports falls. This may mean tightening fiscal policy (e.g. by raising taxes) or monetary policy (e.g. by raising interest rates).

The problem with these policies is that they only provide a short term solution and do not tackle the underlying causes of any persistent current account deficit. They also reduce aggregate demand and this will result in lower economic growth and higher unemployment.

(2) Expenditure switching

Expenditure switching policies are policies that attempt to encourage consumers to switch their demand away from imports and towards the output of domestic firms. This occurs if the **relative price** of domestically produced goods can be lowered. Policies that might achieve this goal include: The introduction of tariffs; policies that reduce the rate of inflation; measures that reduce unit labour costs of domestic firms making their output relatively cheaper (e.g. supply side policies to raise investment and increase labour productivity); a devaluation or depreciation of the exchange rate.

The Marshall-Lerner condition (evaluation)

An **exchange rate depreciation** will not necessarily improve the current account position. An improvement in the current account requires that the value (*not* volume) of exports rises relative to imports, and whether this occurs depends on the elasticity of demand for exports (e_x) and imports (e_m).

The Marshall-Lerner condition states that a depreciation will improve the current account only if the elasticities of demand for imports and exports sum to greater than one:

$$e_x + e_m > 1$$

The J-curve effect (evaluation)

Elasticity of demand for imports and exports is likely to be low in the short term following a depreciation. This is because importers and exporters are tied in by existing contracts. In the long term, they can adjust to exchange rate changes when new contracts are signed. This means that the current account is likely to deteriorate in the immediate aftermath of an exchange rate depreciation (because the **Marshall-Lerner condition** is not satisfied) but may improve in the longer term when traders have had more chance to react. This produces a **J-curve effect** as shown in Figure 28.4.

Figure 28.4: The J-Curve

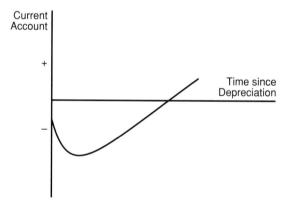

Chapter

29

Unit 4: Measuring the macroeconomy → How the macroeconomy works →
Macroeconomic performance → Macroeconomic policy tools → **International Economics**

Limits to Growth and Development

Growth and Development

Economic growth and **economic development** are closely linked, but are not the same thing. Michael Todaro identified three objectives of development:

- **To increase the availability, and widen the distribution, of basic life sustaining goods.** This relates to the provision of the basic human needs (food, drink, clothing, warmth, shelter and sanitation).
- **To raise standards of living.** This may primarily mean material living standards, but consideration should also be given to non-material factors, amongst which Todaro identifies self-esteem as especially important.
- **To expand the range of economic and social choices.** This objective should be taken to include political freedoms.

Economic growth can lead to wider gains in terms of development. However, all too often the gains from economic growth are concentrated in the hands of just a small section of the population. This leads to a highly unequal distribution of income and wealth and limited economic development. There may be some 'trickle down effects' as spending by the wealthy creates employment opportunities for others, but the pace of development does not match the rate of economic growth.

The main factors limiting growth and development are outlined below:

A lack of saving

High levels of **saving** are important for growth and development because savings provide funds that can be borrowed by firms for **investment** purposes.

In the **Harrod-Domar** model, an economy's rate of growth depends on:

- The proportion of national income that is saved.
- The productivity of the investments undertaken. This can be increased by **technological advances**.

Injections of finance from other countries could be used to offset any shortfall in domestic saving. Even high levels of saving may be insufficient to generate growth if savings are deposited with financial institutions abroad (**capital flight**), or if there are problems in channelling funds to those who wish to borrow for investment purposes.

A lack of savings may create a **poverty trap**. Those who are poor are unable to sacrifice current consumption in order to make savings. This serves to limit the funds available for investment, thus preventing economic growth and trapping countries in poverty.

External finance can bridge savings gaps in developing countries and can come from a number of sources. These include:

- Foreign direct investment by multinational corporations.
- Foreign aid (Official Development Assistance).
- Worker remittances (money sent home by natives of a country who have emigrated to other countries).

A lack of external finance

There has never been enough external finance to have a decisive impact on development. Reasons for this include:

- The fear that corrupt governments would misuse funds.
- Concerns about encouraging aid dependency. This occurs when developing countries require a continual flow of aid and never reach the point where they no longer need outside help.

A narrow economic structure

Many developing countries have a **narrow economic structure**, perhaps focusing on one product or on one sector of the economy. For example, Malawi derives a quarter of its annual income from tobacco leaves.

This creates a number of problems. These include:

- Vulnerability to the effects of disease or weather.

- Exposure to long term price falls as the global supply of many commodities increases due to higher productivity.
- Diminishing marginal returns will occur, as large quantities of labour are employed in combination with limited amounts of land and capital equipment.
- The danger of soil degradation due to over-cultivation. This will reduce output in future time periods.
- Unfair competition from developed countries. Many developed nations give subsidies to their own producers in the primary sector and this gives them an unfair advantage in world markets.
- The limited potential for agricultural commodities to be a source of economic growth. This suggests that development will be difficult unless there is diversification into the secondary sectors.

Geography

Landlocked countries face higher transport costs when trading and this is a significant constraint on growth and development. Geography can hinder development in other ways too. For example a dry climate that is not conducive to food production, or a tropical climate that favours the spread of diseases such as malaria.

Corruption

There are many ways in which corruption can hinder development. These include:

- Money may be embezzled by government officials rather than being spent on public services or investment. This can discourage potential donors from offering aid.
- Scarce resources will not be allocated efficiently when the basis for allocation is bribes to government officials.
- Corruption may include the seizure of property. Market incentives cannot function properly in the absence of property rights.
- Governments may spend money in ways that further their political ends. For example, the stockpiling of weapons.

Population growth

Population growth can help to support economic growth by increasing the availability of labour sources. However, if population increases faster than GDP, per capita GDP falls. Further problems occur when a country begins to develop and its death rate declines. This will create an ageing population that needs to be supported.

Population growth may also have environmental consequences including **resource degradation** (e.g. declining soil quality) and **resource depletion** (e.g. deforestation).

Disease

Diseases including malaria, tuberculosis, and HIV/AIDS are highly prevalent in some developing countries, notably in Sub-Saharan Africa. The results include:

- Increased death rates and reduced life expectancy.
- Health care costs imposed on households. There is an opportunity cost to households as they will have to sacrifice spending in other areas to support sick relatives.
- Sufferers may be unable to work or cannot work as effectively as before.
- Strain on healthcare systems, e.g. resources used for treating diseases like malaria and HIV/AIDS are diverted away from providing other treatments.
- By reducing the labour force, disease reduces the capacity of the economy and limits economic growth. The loss of highly skilled workers is particularly damaging.

War

A feature common to many, but not all, less developed countries is vulnerability to armed conflicts. It is not difficult to see ways in which armed conflict may damage development. These include:

- The destruction of physical capital during the course of the conflict.
- The diversion of labour resources from production to fighting.
- The death of valuable labour resources, some highly skilled.
- The diversion of investment to military capital.
- A loss of confidence deterring investment.
- A loss of vital institutions, such as banks, which are likely to pull out of war torn countries.

Chapter

30

Unit 4: Measuring the macroeconomy → How the macroeconomy works →
Macroeconomic performance → Macroeconomic policy tools → **International Economics**

Promoting Growth and Development

Finance for growth and development

Growth and development require finance. This can come from a number of sources, including:

● **Domestic saving.** The importance of saving is stressed in the **Harrod-Domar model** (see Chapter 29). Policies to encourage saving, such as tax relief on interest earned, may promote growth and development. Alternatively, governments may choose to tax high income earners and use the tax revenue to fund investment.

● **Aid** from foreign governments or charities.

● **Foreign direct investment** from multinational corporations. Developing countries may be attractive locations for multinationals because they offer a source of cheap labour and tend to be more loosely regulated than developed countries.

Government or market led growth and development?

There is likely to be a significant role for governments in promoting economic development. This is especially true in the poorest countries, where many of **the pre-conditions for the effective functioning of markets** may not be in place. These include:

● **Adequate infrastructure.** Good roads and a well functioning transport system are vital if goods are to be transported to their final destination. High quality airports and shipping ports are also required, along with well developed communication networks (telephone and internet provision is now crucial in global markets). It is difficult to see how the market could provide such an infrastructure in very poor countries. For example, private companies will not build roads unless they can make profits from them, but this will not be possible unless a flourishing market system is already up and running.

● **Well functioning financial institutions.** In a market economy, investment depends on **financial intermediaries** such as banks channelling funds from those who wish to save to those who wish to borrow. The state may need to create and maintain a banking system.

● **Protection of property rights.** Entrepreneurs are only likely to invest in what they legally own when they are confident that the law will protect their ownership.

● **Entrepreneurial culture.** The incentive of individual gain may clash with the cultures of many developing countries making it difficult for market activity to flourish.

● **Stability.** Markets require a relatively stable macroeconomic climate in order to function well. For example, inflation must be low and fairly predictable. Governments wishing to promote market led development need to pursue policies that create macroeconomic stability.

However, there are significant advantages if markets, rather than governments, are used to encourage growth and development. These include:

● Governments may fail to make good choices concerning resource allocation and investment. For example, government failure may occur due to a lack of information about the effects of the investment. There may also be conflicting political priorities and potential corruption.

● Where governments are responsible for production, waste is common. There is likely to be x-inefficiency.

● The total level of investment may be higher when it is motivated by the opportunity to make profits in a market economy where enterprise is encouraged.

| Balanced and unbalanced growth | **Balanced growth theory** suggests that it is essential that simultaneous expansion takes place in a wide range of industries, particularly in the early stages of development. Firms and industries need **backward linkages** (to suppliers) and **forward linkages** (a market for their output). If such linkages do not exist, then stagnation is likely. Balanced growth theorists tend to believe that very substantial government intervention is required to promote development. |

Unbalanced growth theory suggests that it is necessary to prioritise growth in some key sectors of the economy because there is a finite amount of resources available for investment. Stimulating growth in certain sectors may create market incentives for entrepreneurs to set up businesses in backward and forward linked industries.

| Industrial-isation | Many developing economies have economies very narrowly focused on agriculture and the primary sector. The economic growth experienced by today's richest countries was based on **industrialisation** (diversification into the secondary sector). This experience is shown in Rostow's stages of growth model: |

Figure 30.1: Rostow's stages of growth model

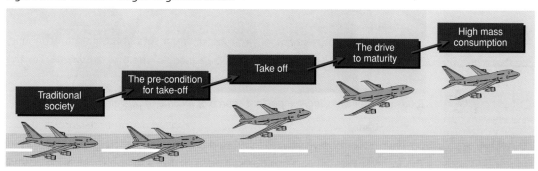

Traditional society	Pre-conditions for take off	Take off	Drive to maturity	High mass consumption
Subsistence agriculture.	Agriculture becomes mechanised and output traded. Transport system develops. Savings and investment grow.	Industrialisation. Manufacturing grows and employment in agriculture falls. Savings and investment grow to around 10-15% of GDP.	Growth becomes self sustaining and spreads to all parts of the country. Industry diversifies. Technology improves.	Output levels are high and mass consumption occurs. The tertiary (service) sector grows.

Many countries have achieved rapid growth through industrialisation. China is the most prominent example, along with other Asian economies such as Singapore. Strategies focused on industrialisation are likely to concentrate on areas that lend themselves to labour intensive production. Industrialisation does carry some costs, such as the disruption to established ways of life and the fact that inequality tends to grow. In many countries, rural communities may be left behind as industrialisation gathers pace.

| Inward looking development policies | **Inward looking development policies** focus on the nation's domestic economy. A classic example is **import substitution**. Import substitution normally occurs in the markets for labour intensive products, such as clothing and footwear. There is a high demand for such products in developing countries that, before industrialisation, is met by imports. Development may focus on replacing these imports with domestically produced goods. This can be achieved by protecting domestic industries from foreign competition. There are, however, some factors that will limit the success of import substitution. Once all imports have been replaced, the potential gains of the policy will be exhausted. It may also be difficult for industries sheltered from competition to become fully efficient and to compete in international markets. |

Tourism is an increasingly important source of income for developing countries.

Outward looking development policies

Governments pursuing **outward looking development policies** are likely to favour an '**open economy**'. This involves dismantling protectionist barriers. It may also involve removing obstacles to the international mobility of labour and encouraging investment from multinational companies. Such openness does leave developing countries exposed to exploitation by multinational firms. This problem is discussed in Chapter 24. Developing countries may suffer a 'brain drain' if their most talented workers are free to leave for higher wage countries.

Tourism

Tourism is an increasingly important source of income for developing nations and many governments are actively promoting tourism as a development strategy. Governments have set up tourist marketing boards that target the citizens of rich developed nations.

The promotion of tourism draws on the biggest asset of many developing countries, namely their environment. The labour intensive nature of tourism makes use of the plentiful labour force supply enjoyed by many developing nations. It injects finance (export earnings) into the circular flow of income, and creates local multiplier effects. The infrastructure created for the tourist industry may benefit the wider economy.

The costs of promoting tourism include the negative externalities that are created. These include the effect of hotel and road construction on scenery and wildlife habitats, and the effect of commercialisation on local cultures.

'Quick wins' in development

More modern development theory concentrates on the efficiency of development spending. It focuses on ways of making quick, substantial advances in development for a low cost. Many examples of such policies come from the area of health. For example, the distribution of insecticide treated bed nets to those living in areas with endemic malaria has had a substantive impact on development.

Appendix 2

Key Macroeconomic Diagrams Summary

Aggregate supply as production costs fall

Figure A2.1

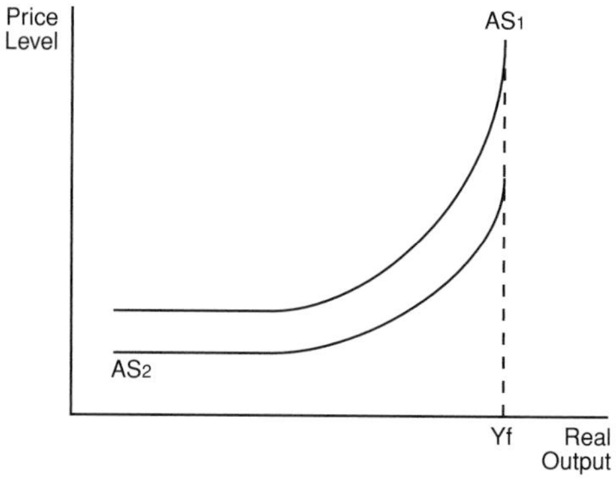

Aggregate supply as capacity increases

Figure A2.2

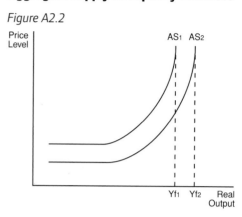

Short run aggregate supply as production costs fall (for AQA)

Figure A2.3

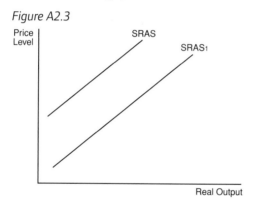

Long run aggregate supply as capacity increases (for AQA)

Figure A2.4

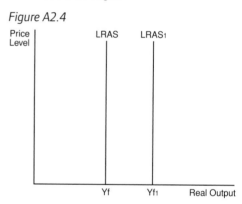

Shifts of AD produce trade-offs

Increasing AD

Figure A2.5

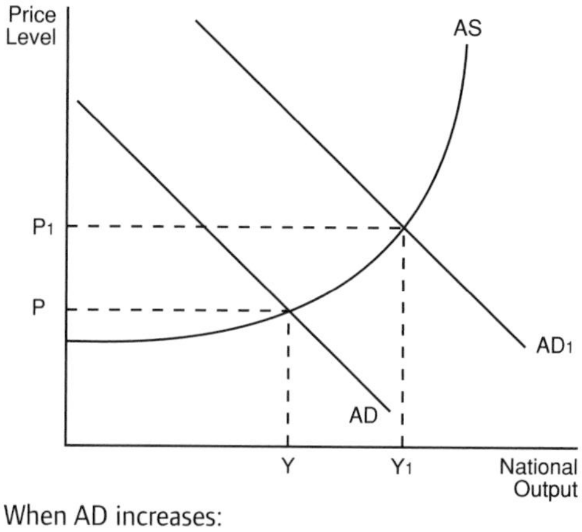

When AD increases:

- Increased output and reduced unemployment.

But

- Inflationary pressure and deterioration of the current account of the balance of payments.

Falling AD

Figure A2.6

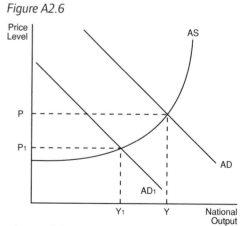

When AD falls:

- Reduced inflationary pressure and improved current account of balance of payments.

But

- Lower output and higher unemployment.

Shifts of AS may move all four main indicators in the same direction

Increasing AS

Figure A2.7

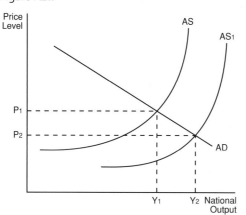

- Potential simultaneous improvement in all four main macroeconomic indicators.

Falling AS

Figure A2.8

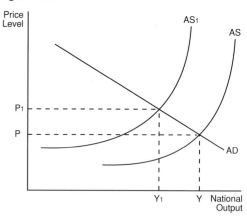

- Potential simultaneous deterioration in all four main macroeconomic indicators.

No long run trade-offs between economic objectives

Increase in AD

Figure A2.9

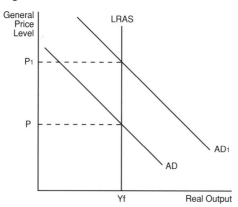

An increase in AD **fails** to increase output and reduce unemployment in the **long run**, but is inflationary and is likely to lead to a deterioration of the current account of the balance of payments.

Increase in long run AS

Figure A2.10

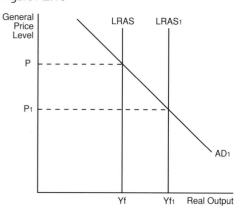

An increase in LRAS is likely to improve all four main economic indicators simultaneously.